LONGING TO BE LOVED

*"Delight yourself in the Lord;
And He will give you the desires of
your heart" (Psalm 37:4).*

ABOUT THE AUTHOR. . .DR. C. S. LOVETT

Dr. Lovett is the president of **Personal Christianity,** a fundamental, evangelical interdenominational ministry. For the past 31 years he has had but one objective—**preparing Christians for the second coming of Christ!** This book is one of over 40 of his works designed to help believers **prepare for His appearing.**

Dr. Lovett's decision to serve the Lord resulted in the loss of a sizable personal fortune. He is well equipped for the job the Lord has given him. A graduate of American Baptist Seminary of the West, He holds the M.A. and M. Div. degrees conferred *Magna Cum Laude.* He has also completed graduate work in psychology at Los Angeles State College and holds an honorary doctorate from the Protestant Episcopal University in London.

A retired Air Force Chaplain (Lt. Colonel), he has been married to Marjorie for over 40 years and has two grown daughters dedicated to the Lord.

ꝈONGING TO BE ꝈOVED

"Delight yourself in the Lord;
And He will give you the desires of
your heart" (Psalm 37:4).

by C. S. Ꝉovett

M.A., M. Div., D.D.

president of Personal Christianity Chapel

author of fifteen best selling books including:
Latest Word on the Last Days
Dealing With The Devil
Soul-Winning Made Easy
"Help Lord — The Devil Wants Me Fat!"

editorial assistance and
illustrated by Linda Lovett

published by:
PERSONAL CHRISTIANITY CHAPEL
Box 549
Baldwin Park, California 91706

3

I'M A TRINITARIAN

In the process of reading this book, you will find
the terms Jesus . . . Father . . . and Lord used interchange-
ably in some places. Please don't let this bother you.
The apostle Paul does the same thing. An outstanding
example can be found in 2 Cor. 3:17 . . . "Now the Lord
is the Spirit." Like you, I am a Trinitarian, believing
in Father, Son and Holy Spirit. Also like you, I believe
the THREE ARE ONE. Therefore it shouldn't be a surprise to find a mingling of the Godhead at some points.
I feel this flows so naturally you probably won't notice
it. But if you should, be assured I would never, in any way,
be disrespectful of our Heavenly Father, the Holy Spirit, or
our Lord Jesus.

PRINTED IN THE UNITED STATES OF AMERICA

ISBN 0-938148-36-2

Contents

"I Love You, Daddy!"

You come home from work and plop in your easy chair. Here comes your little girl, running up and climbing into your lap. She's so happy to see you . . .

"Daddy, I love you. I missed you today. I think you're the best daddy in the whole world. Uummmh daddy, I love you so much!" Smaaacck!

Do you brush aside that affection and send your child away? Of course not. It melts your heart to have your darling express her love so tenderly. Those little arms about your neck . . . that kiss on your cheek . . . communicate an affection that has to move the heart of any father — yes, even our Heavenly Father.

No matter how long we've been saved, you and I are still little children to the Lord. It thrills Him to have us come in childlike faith, showering our affection on Him. And yet, if you visualize God as a pious individual isolated in some heavenly palace, Someone Who insists on being addressed formally and with high-sounding religious words, what I've just said might offend you. Certainly puzzle you. If so, I hasten to apologize.

But you see, this is how I go to God . . . in prayer.

I rush boldly into His presence, put my arms about His neck and tell Him I love Him. Sometimes I'm emotional as I describe what He means to me. It delights Him . . . and it delights me to lavish my affection on Him. If this book accomplishes its purpose, you may find yourself pouring out your affection on Him in the same way. I hope so. That's why I wrote it.

C. S. Lovett

Why I Write
The Way I Do

My parents were divorced when I was a baby, so my grandparents raised me. I grew up without a father. What a vacuum that produced in my soul. I wanted a dad so bad. The yearning was so great I was jealous of almost every kid at school.

When others would speak of good times with their dads, I'd turn green with envy. I was even jealous when they told me how their dads whipped them. If only I had a dad who'd whip me.

At times, I'd fantasize a father who'd take me camping and show me how to do things. I'd picture the two of us sitting alongside a stream while he explained about growing up and how to get along with girls. I ached for a pal like that, someone I could look up to. Someone who'd understand me. Someone I could be proud of.

But alas, it was not to be that way — for a long time. Thirty years passed before the Holy Spirit introduced me to Jesus and I became God's child.

WHAT A FANTASTIC MOMENT

Have you read, **C. S. LOVETT: MARANATHA MAN?** If so, you may recall the peculiar circumstance that led to my salvation. It happened of all places, at a minister's conference. I "accidentally" overheard a conversation between some conference leaders. It was a private discussion as far as they were concerned. But the Holy Spirit meant for me to hear it. They were discussing the mechanics of salvation, focusing on how simple it was for people to be saved.

"If people only knew," offered one of them, "that you can talk directly to Jesus and He hears you."

"Yeah," joined another, "you simply ask the Lord to come into your heart. That's all there is to it. You don't have to beg or meet certain requirements or anything."

9

The third remark really turned the light on for me . . .
"The key to the whole thing is asking the Lord to come into your life and letting Him make Himself real to you!"

I'd heard of salvation in previous years. But I didn't know until that moment what it took to be saved. The mechanics had escaped me. Somewhere along the line I'd missed the process, as simple as it was. But now — in a moment — the whole thing became clear.

● After making the discovery, I rushed home to share the good news with my wife. I remember bursting into the house shouting . . .

"Margie ! Margie ! I found out!"

My darling wife was trying to dry her hands on a towel as I half dragged her into the living room.

"What on earth . . . why are you so excited?" My gushing emotions had her perplexed.

"Just wait until you hear what I found out, honey! You know where I've been wrong all these years?"

"Where, dear?"

"I've been wanting the Lord to make Himself real to me FIRST . . . then I'd put my trust in Him. But it doesn't work that way. I found out you have to invite Him into your heart FIRST, and THEN let Him make Himself real to you!"

WE DID IT TOGETHER

Margie's heart was ready, so we knelt right there

10

in our living room and spoke directly to the Lord:

> "Lord Jesus, we know You hear us, so we're opening
> our hearts to You. We invite You into our lives
> and ask You to make Yourself real to us. We want
> You for our Friend and Savior."

Somehow we both sensed the words we used weren't
all that important. God didn't care HOW we said it.
It was WANTING HIM that counted. Suddenly the
ceiling of the room seemed to open. It was like a
gust of heavenly air sweeping our souls. Margie and
I felt cleansed. We knew He had come into our hearts.
We felt LOVED. I HAD A FATHER, AT LAST.

A FATHER AT LAST

When it struck me that I now had a Father of my
own, I felt a compelling urge to talk to Him. All of
my life I had wanted to call someone "father." Now
I knew what my first words would be . . . "Father,
thank You for wanting me!"

I was still holding Margie in my arms when the
first word came off my lips . . . "Father." But that
was as far as I got. The dam holding back all the longing
in my soul gave way and the pain of years gushed out.

I was so overwhelmed with joy, I couldn't finish
the phrase. I had to say it again. "FATHER!" That
word was so delicious on my lips, I kept repeating. . .
"Father. . .Father. . .Father!"

In my spirit I could feel His response . . . "Yes,
son, you're My boy and I'm your Father!" That sealed
it. I now had a DAD who'd be to me everything I
longed for in an earthly father. The vacuum in my soul
was filled.

11

At last, I finally had a Father of my own. With my Heavenly Father, wife Margie and daughter Linda, my family was complete.

WHY DID IT HAPPEN THIS WAY?

It wasn't too long before it dawned on me why God allowed me to go so long without an earthly father. He wanted me to grow up with that vacuum in my soul, so He could be the One to fill it. That way, He'd be the ONLY FATHER I'd ever know. I mean — real Father.

He knew what He was doing.

Coming to Him as I did . . . desperately needing A PAL . . . it never occurred to me to BE DIGNIFIED with God. My craving overruled that notion. The deep longing for a father with whom I could laugh and play, automatically caused me to brush aside the reverences and pieties people normally attach to God . . . and take HIM as my real Dad. My spirit thought nothing of calling out . . '. "HEY DAD!"

Please don't be offended. You see, I was never exposed to the cliches and high-sounding phrases often used in addressing God. They just never got into my vocabulary. With the Lord taking the place of a **human father**, it was natural for me to think of Him as MY DAD. Though I use non-pious terms in speaking to Him, I don't want you to think for a minute I don't have the greatest respect for Him. He is my God, of course, but also my Dad.

But you know, He's YOUR DAD, too. The Spirit that indwells us when we're saved, moves us to cry out like that . . . "HEY DAD!" Before you object, remember the apostle Paul's teaching on this very point. He said the Spirit in us cries out . . . **"Abba, Father!"** (Rom. 8:15). "Abba" is an Aramaic word meaning "PAPPA!" So I'm not off base. The Holy Spirit plants in each of us a longing to embrace God as our own precious PAPPA! *

HOW GOD CONFIRMED MY FEELINGS FOR HIM

"You know, Sam, you're not the first person to enjoy familiarity with the Lord. Around

---

* If you have not yet asked the Lord Jesus to be your Savior and "Pappa," you could easily take care of it right now. A few simple words, such as those Margie and I said, would do nicely. Or pray like this: **"Dear Jesus, I confess that I'm a sinner, and I here and now open my heart to You. Come into my life, forgive my sins and embrace me as Your child. I want You for my Lord and Savior, and also my Heavenly 'Pappa.' Thank You for loving me. Amen."** If you can do that and mean it, you'll be calling Him "Pappa" too!

300 years ago there was a French monk by the name of Brother Lawrence, who also discovered the secret of intimacy with God."

That was Rev. Leonard Prentice speaking, my first pastor. He was the minister of a small Baptist church not far from my house. Margie and I joined shortly after we were saved.

On this particular day I was in his study, sharing with him how I had come to enjoy the Lord as a constant companion. I spoke of the many things Jesus and I would do together; how we'd sing and chat about little things.

"I think you'd get a real thrill out of reading about Brother Lawrence," he said, rising from his chair. "Let's see, I think I have a copy of that book somewhere in my library. Yes, here it is."

I reached for the small volume he handed me. The title read, **Brother Lawrence: His Letters and Conversations on the Practice of the Presence of God.**

"Hey," I thought to myself, "this ought to be right down my alley."

Pastor Prentice saw my eyes light up. "Let me tell you about this man and then you can read what he has to say about his walk with the Lord."

I SAT BACK AND LISTENED . . .

. . . as Pastor Prentice explained. Lawrence's real name was Nicholas Herman. He was born in Lorraine, a little after 1600, while that area was still a part of France. Though he loved the Lord as a young man, it wasn't until he reached middle age that he became

14

serious about a close walk with Him. Then it was he entered a Carmelite monastary in Paris as a lay brother.

He hoped the monastic life would be a short and sure route to his goal. But as "low man on the totem pole," it fell his lot to scrub the pots and pans after the other brothers of the society had made the mess. It was a detestable assignment. He hated it. He tried to look on it as a means of mortifying his flesh, but that didn't work.

Then something happened.

A change occurred.

In the process of complaining to the Lord about his miserable situation, he began to picture the Lord as listening to his gripes. He began to sense the Lord's sympathy. As he continued this practice, the Lord became more and more real to him. Before long, he was visualizing the Lord as doing the work with him. With the passing of more time, Lawrence and his Lord were laughing about it.

You can guess the result of that. The tiresome task became less and less tiresome. Lawrence soon found himself actually looking forward to scrubbing the pots and pans with Jesus. What was once drudgery became feasts of joy! Lawrence developed a new obsession — a passion for Jesus' presence.

● Lawrence was transformed. No longer was he disappointed with himself. He developed the art of VISUALIZING the Lord Jesus, and it revolutionized his life. He was so caught up with Jesus, so obsessed with Him, that the world and its cares faded from view. So intense was his delight in the Lord, his life radiated a glow people could see. There was a visible effect.

Word of his joy and radiance spread over Europe. Christian royalty journeyed to see him. They hoped to learn the secret of his glowing peace. When asked for his secret, he would say . . .

> **The most excellent method he had found of going to God was that of doing our common business without any view of pleasing men (as far as we're capable,) but purely for the love of God. We ought not to be weary in doing little things for the love of God, Who regards not the greatness of the work, but the love with which it is performed . . . it is enough for me to pick up but a straw from the ground for the love of God.**

THEN I READ FOR MYSELF

The book was not actually written by Brother Lawrence. The Archbishop of Paris learned of this dedicated man and made it a point to get to know him. After numerous conversations with him, he became so impressed with his simplicity, that he would later write down all he could remember of what was said. What I

16

was holding in my hand was a collection of Lawrence's letters written during the last decade of his life. He died in 1691, around the age of 80.

As I skipped through the pages, Pastor Prentice busied himself at his desk. I hadn't read very far when it was obvious Brother Lawrence didn't have much theology. He believed faith took a man further than doctrine. He made it his business to KNOW GOD rather than theology. Had he been a theologian, he might never have dared become so intimate with the eternal God. That was a lesson for me. Theology, as you know, can keep people from doing lots of things with Jesus.

Lawrence's devotional method was simple. **"We should establish in ourselves a sense of God's presence by continually conversing with Him."** In other words, do as Paul ordered . . . "Pray without ceasing." At the same time, the brother knew human weakness and the difficulty of developing the habit of practicing God's presence. In one of his letters, though, he sought to make it easy:

> **"He lays no great burden upon us: a little remembrance of Him from time to time; a little adoration . . . sometimes to offer Him your sorrows, sometimes to return Him thanks for the benefits He has given you. He asks you to console yourself with Him the oftenest you can. The least little remembrance will always be acceptable to Him. You need not cry very loud; He is nearer to us than we think."**

I LIKED THAT

Pastor Prentice was right. I did like the book.

Somehow I sensed a real kinship with Brother Lawrence. Here was a man who knew Jesus as I did and loved Him with the same intimacy. A man who was companion to the Most High God in little things, who made every act of his daily work an act of worship. In his own words . . . "I turn the cake that is frying in the pan for love of Him . . ."

By frequently failing and rising to renewed acts of faith and love, he finally came to the place where he said . . . **"It would be as difficult for me not to think of God, as it was at first to accustom myself to it."** Had Brother Lawrence or myself had much theology, we probably would never have been able to put our arms around Jesus to tell Him how terrific He was.

Brother Lawrence and I were in complete agreement on one thing — the sweetest benefit of practicing the presence of the Lord, is that **you end up with a fabulous Friend** — One Who sees the worst in you and loves you still. Even more, delights in your company. It is glorious to be able to take Him as He is . . . and have Him take you as you are.

As I read the book, it was clear Lawrence and I had reached the same ground. Even though he preceded me by some 300 years, I could almost hear him saying . .

"Go to it brother Lovett. Tell our dear family what it's like to hold Jesus in their arms and be a blessing to Him. I'm sure many long for intimacy with the Lord and would love to feel His everlasting arms about them. If you can lead them into such a relationship, my brother, you'll be doing the saints a great service!"

NOT A NEW TRUTH

What I'm sharing with you is not a new truth, **though**

18

it is one that has been neglected by the modern church. For that reason, it might sound new. The fact is, it has been in operation since Pentecost when the Lord Jesus came to indwell His people via the Holy Spirit. On that day a brand new experience was possible for believers — one announced by the apostle James:

**"DRAW NIGH TO GOD, AND HE WILL DRAW
NIGH TO YOU!"** —James 4:8

That verse is not for the unsaved. It is for believers. It invites Christians to enter into an intimate relationship with the Lord. The poet Emerson caught the intimacy of our union with Jesus . . .

> "Speak to Him for He hears,
>   And spirit with Spirit meet;
> Closer is He than breathing,
>   Nearer than hands and feet!"

● The purpose of this book is to show a person HOW to enjoy the Lord in this exciting way. Having experienced the Lord for myself in this fashion, and coming to Him as I did, my approach is bound to be a bit different. Even so I know the Holy Spirit will make it easy for you to understand . . .

WHY I WRITE THE WAY I DO!

Chapter One

Our Romance With Christ

"I am jealous for you, with a divine jealousy; for I betrothed you to Christ, thinking to present you as a chaste virgin to her true and only husband."
(2 Cor. 11:2 NEB)

Your family is seated around the breakfast table. All, that is, except your teen-age son. He's late in joining the rest of you. The lad is taking an awfully long time getting dressed this morning. Oh, here he comes now. Wow! Does he look different!

You can't believe what you see. "Is this my boy?" you ask yourself. Hair neatly combed. Nails trimmed . . . clothes pressed. And wearing a tie! What's come over him? Ah . . . it doesn't take a wizard to figure out what's happened. Only one thing could produce such an amazing transformation . . . and you know what it is — A GIRL!

What do we have here?

THE TRANSFORMING POWER
OF A NEW AFFECTION!

Your boy is caught in the power of a new obsession . . and it has changed him!

IT SHOULD HAPPEN TO US

 "I beseech you therefore, brethren, by the mercies of God, that ye present your bodies a living sacrifice . . . And be not conformed to this world: but be ye TRANSFORMED by the renewing of your mind . . ." (Rom. 12:1,2).

When the apostle Paul speaks of our being TRANS-FORMED by the renewing of our minds, he's referring to the **transforming power of a new affection**. Salvation, you see, is essentially a "LOVE AFFAIR." Not a boy-girl love affair of course, but not all that different either. When we meet Jesus and fall for Him, it is a romantic situation. He loves us and we love Him.

When it finally dawns on us how fabulous He is and the glory of our relationship with Him, we become captivated, obsessed. The more we get caught up in this exciting "affair," the greater our affection. **The greater our affection, the greater our transformation.**

PRETTY ROMANTIC STUFF

Before you give me a puzzled look, think of all the Bible passages alluding to the ROMANCE between Christ and His church. That's us. **"I have espoused you to Christ,"** says Paul (2 Cor. 11:2). That's engagement talk. Consequently the Christian life is essentially AN ENGAGEMENT. Beyond that, the apostle John looks to the day when the **"bride has made herself ready,"** visualizing our coming wedding (Rev. 19:7).

The Word, it appears, insists you and I and Jesus were "MADE FOR EACH OTHER." We're sweethearts. When a man comes to Christ, the Lord gets as excited as Adam when he first saw Eve. Remember the enthusiasm of the first man? "This is now bone of my bones," he exclaimed, "and flesh of my flesh!" (Gen. 2:23). That's how the Lord feels when we're saved!

WE'VE ALL BEEN THERE

Years ago I was a grocery clerk for Safeway. One day I glanced up from between the cabbages and potatoes. Wow! There she was! "What a terrific girl!" I whispered to myself. In a flash I forgot my vegetables and was at her side, asking if I could be of help. That was the way my relationship with Margie began. It wasn't long before I discovered she was everything a man could want in a wife.

"If someone like that would fall in love with me," I fantasized, "I'd be the happiest man in the world." She seemed so perfect, yet somehow unreachable. I didn't think I had a chance. But the day came when I had the courage to whisper my love for her. Oh boy, did the bells ring when she replied, "I love you, too." My heart did flip-flops. I was head-over-heels in love.

You can see why my heart skipped a beat when I first laid eyes on Margie.

You've been there. You've savored those delirious feelings. You know how consuming they are. Everything changes. You want to be with her all the time . . . do everything together. Thoughts of her occupy your mind to the place where all else has to beg for attention.

THAT'S HOW IT IS WITH JESUS AND US

Remember when you first came to the Lord? How precious it was? You yielded to the Spirit's wooing and opened your heart to Him. His love for you was so overpowering, you adored Him on the spot. Sensing His passion for you, your heart was captured.

Well, that first flush of salvation, that overpowering joy of sins forgiven, that thrill in your soul — AN-NOUNCED your engagement to Jesus. Or, in Paul's words, that's when you were "ESPOUSED" to Him. Then what? As with any engagement, the passing of time allows you to get to know the one to whom you're engaged. I mean **really know** him.

It's like that with Jesus and us.

The longer we know Him, the more we discover how fabulous He is. In time, we're astonished to find Someone so precious and gracious really exists — and wonder of wonders, is in love with us!

IN LOVE. The Bible speaks of 3 kinds of love: 1. phileo (brotherly love), 2. eros (carnal, sexual love), 3. agape (divine, selfless love). In describing our relationship with Jesus as a "love affair," I am referring to AGAPE LOVE, that GIVING LOVE which is all but blind to the faults of another. In our earthly walk we quickly become acquainted with the first two kinds of love. But it is a brand new experience for us to meet someone who loves us with **agape love,** heavenly love, and be joined to that person in an eternal relationship. So new is it, that it takes

24

time for us to discover what it means to be loved with that kind of love. In speaking of our "engagement" to the Lord, I do not wish to imply that any sort of CARNAL love exists between us and Him. Please do not read that into my words.

● When I was first saved, I found myself singing, *"Sweeter as the years go by."* But the words didn't really register. No years had gone by. I couldn't possibly know how wonderful Jesus was, and the degree of His love for me. But with the passing of time, the truth of that song began to dawn on me.

SWEETER AS THE YEARS GO BY

Ever try advising young couples that are about to be married? You might as well save your breath. They haven't the foggiest notion of what you're talking about. Without actual experience, it's a jumble of meaningless words. At this point I could rattle off a list of astonishing qualities describing the most amazing Individual anyone could know. But what would they mean to you?

Well, why don't I do it? That way you'll see what I mean. See if this description makes any sense to you. I'm going to describe Someone Who's really totally unlike anyone you know ...

SOMEONE HOLY AND TRUE... FAITHFUL AND JUST . . . MERCIFUL AND KIND AND GENEROUS. A PERSON WITH UNLIMITED PATIENCE AND UNBELIEVABLY LONG-SUFFERING. ABSOLUTELY IMPARTIAL, WITH NO FAVORITES WHATEVER. SOMEONE WHO NEVER CHANGES HIS MIND ABOUT ANYTHING AND HAS NO UP-AND-DOWN MOODS.

Just words, right? And yet you know Whom I'm describing. **Jesus, the changeless, almighty, eternal God.**

When it comes to being faithful and dependable, you know He's a solid rock. But again, what does a list of words like that mean? They can't mean a thing until you experience them. Until you've actually had Jesus treat you this way, thrilled to His patience and understanding, can you possibly fathom the wonder of His nature.

I'm talking about Someone who never loses His temper, never gets upset when we're mean and nasty. Never reacts, though we persist in selfishness and indifference to His will. Someone Who never displays a speck of anger, even when we keep on doing the same awful things year after year. No matter how terrible the scenes in our imaginations, He never causes us to feel harsh condemnation.

Haven't you found Jesus to be like that? I know you have. We're discussing Someone so blessed, He'll forgive you for the SAME SIN 1000 times a day. And when He comes to the 1000th time, He forgives as wholeheartedly as He did the first time . . . with no hint of exasperation. Jesus FORGIVES WITHOUT CEASING, erasing our guilts so completely, that we forget by afternoon the sins we committed that very morning. I know that's your experience. Never for a moment do we feel He holds anything against us.

● Here's a father teaching his child to walk. The toddler takes a few steps . . . and oops . . . down he goes. Does the father give up? Does he quit? No, he starts the infant off again. Down he goes again. Is that father keeping score on all those falls? No way. He's too excited over the fact 'that his child is learning to walk.

When a child is learning to walk, it is not the number of times he falls down that counts, but the steps he takes. It is his progress that pleases his parents.

And so with God.

Regardless of the way some picture God, He is NOT legalistic. He isn't standing there with a fly swatter, just waiting for us to sin so He can swat us. He is not waiting to judge us. He's a Father, not a lawyer. He doesn't keep track of the times we fall down. **He's interested only in the progress.**

The Lord is our Father, not a lawyer. It helps to picture Him as a Father teaching His child to walk. It is not the number of times the child falls down that counts, but the steps he takes that please God.

NOTHING BETWEEN

"Nothing between my soul and the Savior." I would guess you've sung those words a few times. It's a grand old hymn. And it's true, the Lord won't allow anything to come between us and Him — including our sins. I'm not suggesting for a second that He approves of sin. That'd be ridiculous. He hates sin. It took Jesus' death to redeem us from its curse. Even so, God knows we're still sinners and has provided for it . . .

 "If we confess our sins, He is faithful and just to forgive us our sins, and to cleanse us from all unrighteousness." (1st John 1:9 KJV)

Ah, look what just popped up. **God's faithfulness.**

Have you considered that the forgiveness of our sins is based on God's faithfulness? To Whom is He faithful? Jesus. Think how unjust it would be if the Lord were to die for our sins and then have God refuse to forgive them. Why He would never do that. Observe then, how our continuing fellowship with Jesus is based on God's faithfulness, not on our godliness.

See what that means? Sin cannot ruin our fellowship with God — **as long as we confess it.** We need never be afraid of what Jesus sees in us. The filthy slate is erased when we acknowledge our sins:

 "Yes Lord, I agree with you. This sin is awful. I hate it. And I side with you against it. Please help me to overcome it."

When we do that, it's as though we had not sinned at all.

KNOW ANYONE ELSE LIKE THAT?

Ever met anyone else who forgives the SAME SINS again and again with not the slightest sign of impatience? You just don't find people like that. They're not around. Yet, our Jesus is like that. Let me ask: is it possible to appreciate this amazing grace simply by reading the Bible. No. You have to be forgiven again and again to know such sweetness. You have to EX-PERIENCE IT.

WHY is our Lord like this? He can't help Himself. It's his NATURE to forgive. **He's a forgiver.** That's the way He is. There isn't a speck of unforgiveness in Him.

Now if He were no more than that, our Lord would

28

still be the most fantastic person who ever lived. But He IS more than that. He is also **gentle** and **generous**.

What's more, He knows BY EXPERIENCE the power of our flesh, and how weak it makes us. Instead of judging us, He pities us. This is why He never deals with us harshly. When you come right down to it, He'd have every reason to wipe us out — and be justified — for the awful things we DO, SAY and THINK. But He doesn't. Instead He showers great kindness upon us.

Now you've got to admit that's a SUPER PERSON. But again, it's because He can't help Himself. He's a giver — BY NATURE. It is not in Him to withhold good things from those who love Him (1 Cor. 2:9).

But what of **His patience?**

This is so precious. Have you noticed the way the Lord waits YEARS for us to make even the slightest changes? **The one thing He seeks more than anything else, is for us to BE LIKE HIM.** Yet we go year after year with little growth, little change. Fact is, we resist change. We even resent the circumstances He arranges to change us. And we express our resistance with such phrases as . . . "Don't make waves. Don't rock the boat!" We want things to stay just as they are — ourselves included.

But does He get upset? No. He just waits . . . year after year . . . looking for the tiniest change, the tiniest effort on our part. Though it pains Him to see us living so far below our potential, He patiently bides His time. Instead of getting upset with us, He bears it sweetly — and suffers with us.

No wonder the Bible says, "No one is good except God alone" (Mk. 10:18 NAS). The Lord Jesus is so gracious in all of His ways, all others look bad by comparison.

29

I hope I don't weary you, telling how precious Jesus is. I want you to grasp the dearness of our magnificent Lord. You'll see why in a bit. There are things about Jesus that just won't quit.

His impartiality, for example. **Jesus has no favorites.**

Now that's remarkable. Here's what it means to you. He doesn't love Moses or Billy Graham more than He loves you. You're as precious to Him as anyone else.

Sometimes we're tempted to think our sins are so awful He couldn't possibly love us with the same passion as those who seem more holy and obedient. And when you find yourself repeating the same sins again and again, you don't see how He could love you as fervently. But there's no way for Jesus to be partial. He would NOT BE HOLY if he played favorites. **His holiness guarantees He loves you equally with all other Christians.**

CLOSER THAN A BROTHER

 " . . . there is a friend that sticketh closer than a brother!" (Prov. 18:24 KJV)

A young girl excitedly came to me with the news that she was in love with a lad in my congregation. On an impulse I checked with his mother. "I hope this girl isn't taking him too seriously," said the mother. "Jim falls in love with a new girl every month."

Men are like that. Fickle, falling in love and out of love easily. BUT NOT GOD. When He loves, He commits Himself. From then on, NOTHING can change the way He feels. When He says, **"Never will I leave you; never will I forsake you,"** He means it (Heb. 13:5 NIV). He sticks like glue. And when He comes to dwell in our hearts . . . it's for KEEPS (Rom. 8:38,39; John 10: 27-29).

Think about that. **What could be more glorious than having a personal friend as committed to you as Jesus!** Did you know He literally ACHES for fellowship with you, considering you so dear to Him, He'd die for you! When someone as sweet as the Lord Jesus is willing to take you AS YOU ARE, how can you lose? And on top of that, He lives to bring you to your best! It's almost too much for the heart to hold.

As the famous Mr. Kingsley once said:

> *"A friend is a soul whom we can trust utterly: who knows the best and the worst in us, and loves us in spite of our faults. He is someone who will give us counsel and reproof in the day of prosperity and self-conceit, but will also comfort us and encourage us in the days of difficulty and sorrow. He never gets in our way, except when we're on the way down. And then he stands between us and the bottom."*

No wonder it gets sweeter as the years go by.

IT'S ROMANTIC OBSESSION

I met Glen Allen in high school. It wasn't a close friendship, because he had "radio fever." I'm using that term to describe his obsession. He was into amateur radio.

Glen had a "ham" station in his garage. He was totally caught up in the thrill of short wave contact with foreign countries. He spent every spare minute in that garage. Every dime he could scrape up went into his equipment. His mother had to drag him to the dinner table. After

31

the family was asleep, he'd sneak out at night to spend more hours "working his rig."

When I wanted to see Glen, I knew where to find him — in the garage. He was never any place else, except school. Even there he didn't mix with the other kids, his head was always buried in a radio manual. All he could think of was radio. Were it not for my casual interest in radio, time with him would have been a bore. The lad was totally obsessed.

Glen's obsession reminds me of the apostle Paul's passion . . ."**For me to live is Christ!**" he said (Phil 1:21). "**This one thing I do**," he affirmed (Phil 3:13). He was infatuated with Jesus. Obsessed to the place where only one thing mattered — **exalting Christ!**

We should be as obsessed with Christ as Glen was with his ham radio.

• Remember the lad who was late to breakfast? His life was changed because of a new obsession — A GIRL. The same should be true of us as we fall more and more in love with Jesus. When we discover how remarkable He is, we can easily become obsessed with Him. That's why I dwelt so long on His matchless character. As a Person, He's absolutely delicious!

DELICIOUS!

When our two girls were little, Margie and I got a big kick out of bathing them. Once we had them all dried and powdered, we'd pick up our "wigglies" and hold them close to us. They'd smell so good. Then we'd squeeze them against our chests and kiss them, saying . . . **"Uuuuummmmh, I could eat you up!"**

You know what I mean. You've done the same. You've said similar things when you lovingly crushed your own children to your heart. Even as you squeezed them tightly, you wished there were a way to get even closer. Well, that's how I feel about Jesus. I could "eat Him up!" He's truly delicious!

Ah — but how does He feel about us? We haven't said much about that. We took a close look at His matchless character, His unbelievable grace. We've thrilled to the fact that He sees EVERYTHING that goes on inside us and still wants us. There is nothing hidden from His eyes. Our most selfish, prideful and filthiest thoughts are laid bare before Him (Heb. 4:13). But wonder of wonders in spite of beholding the worst in us — He still loves us.

What kind of love is that? We'll see—next.

Chapter Two

Jesus -
The "World's
Greatest Lover!"

"For God so loved the world, that He gave His only begotten Son, that whosoever believeth in Him should not perish, but have everlasting life." (John 3:16 KJV)

"World's greatest lover!"   That's me . . . and I've got the trophy to prove it.   The occasion was our wedding anniversary. We both laughed when my wife Margie presented it to me. It was a big joke. But the male ego being what it is, I didn't throw it away. Right this moment, it stands in plain view on a shelf in my book case. I haven't paid much attention to it in recent years — until I was working on this chapter.

The Holy Spirit kept drawing my eyes like a magnet to the words, "World's Greatest Lover!" Immediately I knew what He had in mind. He wanted me to understand that **only one person deserves that title — our wonderful Lord Jesus. He's the "World's Greatest Lover!"**

Have you ever thought of the Lord that way? He is indeed a lover. So much so, the Bible says,**"God is love"** (1 John 4:8). Believe it or not, He's "head-over-heels" in love with you! He's "hooked" on you, bound by an unmovable passion that won't let go. Every time we sing, *"O Love That Wilt Not Let Me Go,"* we're testifying to the consuming passion He has for you.

LOVERS HAVE A BIG PROBLEM

Lovers need someone to love. What could be more awful than a lover with no one to love? Can you imagine the pain, the emptiness, the ache that would create? Consider then, our Lord. **As a God of love, He NEEDS someone to love. That's why He made us in His own image. He needed someone LIKE HIMSELF on whom He could lavish His love . . . and be loved in return.**

Some think it's absurd to believe God takes a **personal** interest in us. We're such tiny creatures, they say. Why should He care about us? We live in a universe so expansive it cannot be measured with radio telescopes, and so microscopic it cannot be plumbed with electronic microscopes. Why then, they ask, would God want a personal relationship with us? What would be the point?

Ah—faith allows us to believe God's Word when it says this entire world was made for us! He designed it as a place where we could come to know Him BY FAITH. Yes, even fall in love with Him to the place where He becomes our DEAREST FRIEND.

HOW GOD EARNED HIS TROPHY

Most people think God needs but snap His fingers and everything is the way He wants it; that this goes with being God. Well, it's not that easy. The Lord went to a lot of trouble to have you and me.

It's quite a story.

Before there was a physical world with anyone in it, God in heaven needed A COMPANION to love. So He created one. That was accomplished with the snap of a finger. Lucifer, that's his name, was endowed with the freedom of choice, so that he could return God's affection for him if he wanted to. But something went wrong.

Lucifer, as you know, had ideas of his own. He not only didn't return God's love, he thought he should BE GOD! So with his free will he masterminded an angelic revolt, thinking to seize God's throne by a coup! He failed, of course, and so did the FINGER SNAPPING method of creating loving companions for God. The Bible says SIN began with Lucifer's rebellion, the day iniquity was found in him (Ezek. 28:12-17).

What would God do? There was no way He could tolerate sin in heaven. To have evildoers in that place would be an offense to His holiness. So God banished Lucifer (also called Satan) and his followers from His presence (Isa. 14:12-15). A place described as "everlasting fire" was created as the final destiny of these disobedient rebels (Matt. 25:41). The fallen angels came to be known as DEMONS.

36

THE LUCIFER PROJECT DIDN'T WORK

But then God did a strange thing. He did not immediately cast Satan and his band of fallen angels into hell. Instead, He permitted them to roam about the spirit world. Obviously He could have exterminated them in a flash, but God was too wise for that. Now that sin was found in His kingdom, He now had something He didn't have before. Why throw it away when He could make GOOD USE of it?

The rebellion, nonetheless, was a tragedy in one sense. It left God without a friend. He still needed someone to love. How would He fill the void? Ah — here's where we see the genius of our Heavenly Father. With sin in His kingdom, He could come up with a brand NEW METHOD of producing friends and lovers. It was an astonishing concept — HE'D REPRODUCE HIS OWN LIKENESS. He'd create beings after His OWN IMAGE.

> **TRAGEDY.** I hasten to qualify the word, "tragedy." To say that Satan's rebellion left God without a friend is indeed true. And that, in a sense, is tragic. But in another sense, there are no tragedies with God. Because of His genius, our Heavenly Father can make ANY SITUATION (whether in His life or ours) fit His plan perfectly. On the surface it appears the Lucifer experiment failed. However, from what we know of God's FOREKNOWLEDGE, it is better to assume God knew Lucifer would rebel. Then, as soon as that happened, He had a NECESSARY TOOL for bringing forth the kind of companions He really wanted. That tool was SIN.

A TERRIFIC IDEA

With SIN present in His kingdom, God would USE IT to bring forth a race of TESTED LOVERS! He could test them with sin. That would remove all the risk. That made it possible for God to bring forth the perfect companion — A BEING REPRODUCED FROM HIS OWN ESSENCE AND SUBSTANCE, one just like Himself! Before sin entered the picture, he wouldn't take that risk. But with sin present, He could TEST any kind of creature he brought into being. So God embarked on a plan to REPRODUCE HIMSELF, that is, **bring forth SONS from within His own being!**

What a terrific idea! These would be people capable of loving Him as He longed to be loved. And He could make them totally free, with absolutely free wills — as free to love Him as He was free to love them. This would now be a TRUE LOVE RELATIONSHIP.

But with SIN in the picture, God **would not** put His newly created partners in heaven with Him, as He did Lucifer. Instead, **He'd create a SEPARATE ENVIRON-MENT for them — an environment where they could be TESTED WITH SIN.** That is what the EARTH is all about. If God can test people BEFORE He brings them into heaven, all risk is removed. Those who pass the test qualify for eternity with Him. Those who fail, making the same choice Satan made, share the devil's fate.

SO GOD MADE MAN

Our Lord worked diligently to create a suitable environment for His future lovers, whom he called "MAN." The result was the physical heavens and earth. The early chapters of Genesis describe how carefully He saw to it that everything was "very good," perfect in fact, for the new objects of His love.

As part of the TEST PROCESS, a special "carth suit" was devised for God's image to use for getting about on the earth. Man was placed inside a two-legged vehicle which we call the human body, and his perceptions limited to the FIVE SENSES of that body. In this way, man was CUT OFF from any **spiritual awareness** of God and His glory. All he would know of God was what God elected to reveal about Himself.

CREATION OF ADAM
What a glorious moment when the first man stepped forth from the hand of God!

To the first pair, Adam and Eve, the Lord presented Himself in a **physical form**. This permitted them to know Him and enjoy fellowship with Him on a face to face basis. They still had to BE TESTED. So the test began with Satan being turned loose on Eve. The focal point of the test was the "tree of the knowledge of good and evil" (Gen. 2:9; 3:1-7). Would Eve believe what God said about disobedience and death, or would she believe Satan's accusation that God was a liar?

© Linda Lovett 1979

When the woman saw that the fruit of the tree was good to eat, and that it was pleasing to the eye, she took some and ate it. She also gave Adam some and he ate it.

Eve's decision is famous the world over. **God's first friends succumbed to the devil's deception. Sin had now entered His new creation.** Once again His holiness was offended, so God had to separate Himself from this precious pair. Thus Adam and Eve were banished from the garden and their fellowship with the Lord was severed.

After making tunics of skin for Adam and
his wife, the Lord God cast them out
from the garden of Eden. To the east of
the garden He stationed the cherubim
with a flashing sword to prevent them
from eating from the tree of life (Gen.
3:21-24).

ANOTHER TRAGEDY?

On the surface, yes. From where we sit, the Lord
could have "thrown in the towel" and abandoned the
entire program. You can't help but wonder if that
thought didn't cross His mind. But again, this was no ordinary creation — **this was God's own image!** If He
couldn't make lovers out of them, where would He
turn? What hope would He have for fellowship throughout eternity?

In purely HUMAN terms, I can almost hear God saying to Himself . . .

"No way will I give up on this plan! I'm going to salvage these undeserving people one way or another. I'm so in love with them, I refuse to live without them. If I can't have them, I don't want anyone else. I'd rather die. So, I'm going to provide a way for those who really WANT ME to come to Me. They deserve to die, but I'm going to send MY SON to die in their place, so that those who love Me, can be restored and my plan can continue."

Does God think that way? No, that's the way we might picture His thinking. Again, we have to say God FOREKNEW Adam's fall, even as He foreknew Lucifer's rebellion. But we're right about the redemption price. To keep from compromising His holiness, the death penalty for sin had to be upheld. Since there was no way for man to pay it and remain in fellowship with God, the Lord had to die. **"I'd rather die than be without them!"** That part is true.

HE DID DIE

 "For God so loved the world that He gave His one and only Son, that whoever believes in Him shall not perish but have eternal life" (John 3:16 NIV).

How many of us would sacrifice our precious sons or daughters for a bunch of rebellious sinners, most of whom refuse to have anything to do with us? Only God! So desperate was He for our affection, so completely in love with us, He couldn't let go. **He just couldn't bring Himself to part with us, no matter what it cost Him.** When you consider the price He paid to redeem us, there can be no argument about His obsession.

Behold the ultimate Lover giving the supreme gift! Should you ever find yourself doubting God's passion for you, His absolute determination to have you, His desperate longing for you as His lover, look again to Calvary. The Lord withheld nothing. **He gave the most anyone can give – HE GAVE HIMSELF!**

MIX. See now why I said what I did on the copyright page? You see I mix God and Jesus. Yes, Jesus is the One Who died to make it possible for us to have fellowship with God. But God and Jesus are one. It's as Paul says," . . . God was in Christ reconciling the world to Himself, no longer holding men's misdeeds (sins) against them . . . " (2 Cor. 5:19 NEB). Jesus is God's WAY of bringing us into fellowship with Himself. He is God's unspeakable gift, the ultimate expression of His Love for us! (2 Cor. 9:15).

GOD'S OFFER TO ALL MEN

Jesus' sacrifice makes it possible for God to invite all

men to enjoy fellowship with Him. **The way is now open. Fact is, God even begs men and women everywhere to be reconciled to Him through the death of His Son** (Rom. 5:10; 2 Cor. 5:20,21). When you read these verses you can almost hear God pleading . . .

"Come to Me. It won't cost you anything. I've paid your way. You don't know how much I love you, how much I need you, how much I want you. All I ask is that you WANT ME."

True, He approaches each man differently, because each of us is unique. No two alike. But you would expect that from a God of variety. Just as there are no two snowflakes alike, so does every man differ from every other man. This is what is going to make the heavenly fellowship exciting — our differences.

Thus God reveals Himself in a unique way to every individual. Some need more light . . . and get it. Others require less. Whatever it takes, God sees that every man gets what he needs to be able to place his trust in Him. He is "not willing that any should perish" (2 Peter 3:9).

INSTANT SONS — INSTANT LOVERS

Today, almost everything comes in an instant form... coffee . . . credit . . . etc. God was producing instant sons long before man thought of "jiffy" anything. How? By the FAITH METHOD. As different individuals would encounter the knowledge of God (by whatever means the Lord chose to reveal Himself), they would respond with belief or unbelief. It was up to the Lord to make sure each person received the right amount of revelation so as to make a freewill decision FOR OR AGAINST Him.

Which brings us to Satan's part in the process.

● The devil is free to make overtures to man, also. He can approach men and women as easily as does the Lord. This is what makes it a VALID TEST. The Lord allows Satan to make suggestions to every man and woman, just as he did to Eve. Thus all men are confronted with BOTH God's promises and Satan's temptations. This is how God provides Himself with a family of TESTED LOVERS, proven friends. Even as God pleads with men, the devil whispers . . .

"Don't listen to all that talk about heaven, that 'pie-in-the-sky' stuff. The only life you have is the one you're living right now. So don't blow it. Get all you can for yourself; live every day to the full, for this is all there is. Tomorrow you die. Any talk of life after death is just a fairy tale. You're too smart to fall for anything as stupid as that. So don't listen to any of that Bible talk."

YOU CAN SEE HOW THIS PUTS MAN IN THE MIDDLE. HE CAN ACT ON THE REVELATION HE RECEIVES FROM GOD OR HE CAN LISTEN TO THE DEVIL AND REJECT GOD'S OFFER OF LOVE.

Whenever a man responds to the light God gives him, freely deciding he WANTS the Lord, A MIRACLE TAKES PLACE. God's Spirit unites with that man's spirit. Every human being has a spirit and is a SPIRIT RECEIVER (1 Cor. 2:11). By means of his spirit, any man who desires to do so, may receive the SPIRIT OF GOD. When he does, he becomes a CHILD OF GOD that instant (Rom. 8:9,15,16)!

But that's only part of the miracle.

When a man chooses to love the Lord and receives His Spirit, God puts HIS OWN NATURE in that man.

45

That's right, His very own righteous nature. This makes it possible for the Christian to love God as He longs to be loved. A man with God's nature can love God with the same passion God has for him. Isn't that beautiful? We're talking about a real love union, one the apostle Paul urgently wants us to understand, "He that is joined to the Lord IS ONE SPIRIT" (1 Cor. 6:17). Imagine being ONE SPIRIT with God! This is an inseparable union. Once joined to us, the Lord can no more be separated from us than He can be separated from His own Spirit (Rom. 8:38,39)!

IS IT CLEAR? Here's the situation. Man is made in the image of God. At some point in his life he encounters sufficient revelation of God to be able to decide whether he likes the Lord enough to want Him for a personal friend. He doesn't enjoy a face to face meeting with God, but he does receive enough information for his faith to operate. He learns enough about the Lord to know that He is a fantastic person who'd make a super friend. One, in fact, who's eager to share an astonishing future with him. The Lord says to him . . . "If you'll open your heart to Me, I'll come in" (Rev. 3:20). The man says "Yes, I want You for my Friend and Father. Please come into my life and direct my steps!" Thrilled with that kind of an invitation, the Lord enters the man's heart. The SPIRIT TO SPIRIT UNION occurs and he is instantly a child of God (1st John 3:2)!

● Didn't I tell you God's plan was ingenious? Consider what He's done. By imparting His OWN NATURE to the believer, that man can now love God as He longs to be loved. By this method, God gains for Himself through the SON PROGRAM something that was impossible through the ANGEL PROGRAM. He now has people EXACTLY LIKE HIMSELF, capable of loving Him with the same kind of love He has for them. That guarantees Him a glorious future with HIS OWN.

46

BUT THE ACHE REMAINS

As I write these lines I find myself becoming sensitive to the ache in God's heart. My thoughts pause on the idea of His pleading with men to WANT HIM. I almost think the Holy Spirit is letting me sample something of His passion for men. Imagine someone so gentle and kind, so generous and merciful as our God, begging people to like Him! I feel an ache in my own heart as I picture the yearning in His face. And He's been feeling this for centuries.

The prophet Jeremiah had tears in his eyes most of the time. That's why he's called "the weeping prophet." He knew God's heart, how He craved the affection of His people. See if you don't feel a tinge of the heavenly ache in Jeremiah's words to Jerusalem . . .

 "What fault did your fathers find in Me, that they strayed so far from Me . . . ? (Jer. 2:5 NIV)

Jeremiah lived in a day when Israel and Judah had rebelled against the Lord and gone into awful apostasy. And here is God crying through the prophet, **"What's wrong with Me that you don't want Me?"** It seems unthinkable that anyone would knowingly forsake Him after knowing how good He is. Yet, this is a common occurrence. In our day, God is a nuisance to many, a wet blanket on their fun. For some it would be great news to learn that God REALLY WAS DEAD!

As I sit alone with Him at my typewriter . . . listening to His Spirit . . . I can almost hear Him sobbing . . .

"Why don't people like Me? Why do they reject Me? After all, I love them and have done everything I can to be friends with them. How can they be so cold to-

ward Me after I have given them the best I have — My only Son?"

Who can answer that question? Just think — someone as nice as Jesus, and most of the world will have nothing to do with Him. What an awful thing for God to bear. It's worse when you consider **man alone can satisfy the heart of God.** This is the real human tragedy.

> *Jesus, Who for my transgression*
> *Didst the shameful cross endure,*
> *And didst there the blest possession*
> *Of Thy joys to me insure.*
>
> *Wondrous woes that brought salvation!*
> *Wondrous grace to sinners shown!*
> *Heaven is wrapt in contemplation*
> *Of His love, whom men disown!*
>
> *O my soul! wilt thou disown Him?*
> *Wilt not thou, my heart, enthrone Him?*

ONLY WE CAN SATISFY GOD

When God fashioned man, He didn't design him as a PET. He made him HIS OWN IMAGE, in no way inferior to Himself. You can love pets, but you don't make sweethearts of them. You certainly wouldn't marry one. For God to enjoy a GENUINE ROMANCE, it was necessary that His lovers be like Him in every way. **Nothing less than His own likeness could meet the need of His heart.**

> **ANGELS COULDN'T DO IT.** Some might argue that God has a heaven full of angels ready to give Him all the praise and companionship He needs. But angels are NOT SONS. They could never be more than companions. The fall of Lucifer is proof that God couldn't fully commit Himself to angels. Besides, they are NOT HIS OWN KIND. The Word

48

describes them as SERVANTS who wait on us as "ministering spirits" (Heb. 1:14). **Only to RE-DEEMED SONS (tested sons) can the Lord commit Himself. Only those BORN OF HIM can return His love AS EQUALS.** Equal in nature that is, not in rank. While the angels praise God continually and do His bidding at once, their companionship doesn't compare with the JOY He gets from the love of JUST ONE of His own sons!

NO TROPHY FOR US

"World's Greatest Lover!" Disgust sweeps over me. Some lover I am. That little trophy on my bookshelf is a testimony to false pride. Do you know what I do about God's passion for me? What most Christians do — ignore it, much of the time anyway. Be honest, don't we all ignore Him — a great deal of the time?

The evidence is overwhelming! How much of each day do we spend in His presence? How much time do we devote to His Word? What priority do we give Him in our daily routine? And when we finally turn to Him, isn't it usually because we **want** something? You know it is.

Visit a prayer meeting. Listen as the different ones pray. Take note of the "gimmes" . . . give me this . . . give me that!

How disappointing for God! **After pouring out Himself for us, most of us are more interested in GETTING from Him than in GIVING to Him.** Our family and friends receive better treatment than He does. Is that really fair after all He's done for us and has planned for us? Is it right to treat our precious Lord this way when we know His heart yearns for our fellowship? Of course it isn't.

Someone testified to our neglect with these words:

OUR LONELY LORD

When we call Jesus,
* we call Him collect.*
Once in a while we please Him,
* but mostly we neglect.*
People live for the weekend,
* beginning with Friday night.*
Jesus gets real lonely,
* and He's got a right.*

When we enter His presence,
* we select the time and place.*
Usually it's on Sunday,
* when we want His amazing grace.*
We bow our heads in prayer,
* while our minds are far away.*
What does Jesus really get,
* when we begin to pray?*

People see His picture,
* but usually don't look twice.*
Maybe read their Bibles once a week,
* and think they're super nice.*
Only when we come to the end of our rope,
* do we look to the Lord above.*
Shame on us for making Jesus lonely,
* when we should be giving Him our love!*

We've got to do better by Him . . . right?

MOTIVATED TO DO BETTER

How can I scold you? You don't like our neglect of Jesus any more than I do. It's painful for me to consider how selfish I am where He's concerned. **But it doesn't have to be this way.** Instead of scolding, I'd rather motivate you to pay more attention to Him. How? **By sharing with you a glorious mystery — a way He has provided for each of us to get really close to Him.**

50

Even though our Lord operates in the SPIRIT and we operate in the FLESH, there's a way to enjoy Him that will astound you. You're going to be thrilled when you see how it works. If you can grasp what the Holy Spirit reveals in the next three chapters, you may well find the Lord giving you a trophy . . .

"THE WORLD'S GREATEST LOVER!"

Chapter Three

Closer Than Breathing!

"God is Spirit, and His worshipers must worship in spirit and in truth." (John 4:24 NIV)

The mystery of how God provided for us to receive His Spirit begins with one of the strangest stories of the New Testament.

The Lord Jesus and His disciples had left Jerusalem, traveling a route most Jews avoided. They were headed north to Gallilee, but the Lord deliberately chose to pass through Samaria. The Jews and Samaritans shunned each other like the plague.

As they came to Jacob's well, the Lord was exhausted. He sent His disciples ahead into the village to buy food while He rested at the edge of the well. When the disciples were out of sight, a woman approached, carrying a water jar on her head. She looked at Jesus. He looked at her. His garment identified Him as a Jewish Rabbi.

© Linda Lovett 1974

As she lowered her bucket to draw water, the Lord asked her for a drink. She was stunned.

"You're a Jew and I'm a Samaritan woman. How can you ask me for a drink?"

"If you knew the gift of God and Who it is that asks you for a drink, " answered Jesus, **"you would have asked Him and He would have given you living water."**

To the woman's mind, living water had to do with the spring at the bottom of the well, some 105 feet below the surface. But Jesus, of course, was referring to the water of eternal life that satisfies man's **spiritual** thirst.

"Everyone who drinks of this water will be thirsty again," said Jesus, **"but whoever drinks the water I give him, will never thirst."**

That sounded good to the woman. Still thinking of physical water, she could see how His offer would save her a lot of trips to this well. After all, it was some distance from town and she made her trips in the heat of the day. A prostitute by trade, she couldn't draw water in the cool of the day, for then she'd bump into the respectable ladies of the village.

"Sir," she said eagerly, "give me this water so that I won't get thirsty and have to keep coming here to draw water."

Jesus then told her to go call her husband. Sensing something remarkable in the Rabbi speaking to her, she owned up to the fact that she didn't have a husband. The Lord commended her for speaking the truth and then revealed something startling about her.

"The fact is, you've had five husbands and the man you now have is not your husband."

That did it. Now she knew this was no ordinary man. He was able to look into her life and see her secrets. He had to be at least a prophet. If so, he might be able to settle the centuries old debate between Jews and Samaritans — where is the proper place to worship God?

"Sir." she said, "I can see that you are a prophet. Our fathers worshiped on this mountain (Mt. Gerizim), but you Jews say the temple where God should be worshiped is in Jerusalem (Mt. Zion)."

That touched a nerve in Jesus. Knowing He would one day be indwelling this woman in the Spirit, He laid on her a whopping truth. It's as though her talk about worshiping God IN PLACES caused the great secret to pour out of Him.

"Believe me, woman," He said to her, **"the time is**

54

coming when you will worship the Father neither on this mountain nor in Jerusalem. You Samaritans worship what you do not know. We worship what we do know, for salvation is from the Jews. Yet a time is coming and has now come when the true worshipers will worship the Father in spirit and in truth, for they are the kind of worshipers the Father seeks. God is spirit, and His worshipers must worship Him in spirit and in truth."

So, to a Samaritan woman, a prostitute at that, **Jesus announced the divine worship program was about to be changed** — from EXTERNAL worship of God to INTERNAL.

> **INDWELL.** The fact of Jesus' indwelling is one of the most blessed truths of the New Testament. It was never God's intention that His Son would simply come and die for us . . . and that would be it. His sacrifice for us paved the way for Him to do an amazing thing in us — INDWELL US. That is, **actually live inside us.** While the Bible says a lot about God being in the MIDST of His people and dwelling AMONG them, His desire for INTIMACY goes far beyond the physical relationship. **From the moment God made man, He had in His mind that at some point He would join Himself to those who wanted Him, by actually INDWELLING them.** Knowing all that God had planned, Jesus was fully aware of this as He ministered on earth. When the woman raised the age old question, He chose to let her in on the secret.

To this the woman answered, "I know that Messiah is coming. When He comes, He will explain everything to us."

Then Jesus declared, **"I Who speak to you am He!"** (John 4:4-26 NIV)

Can you believe that scene? Here was Jesus speaking

55

to a foreign woman (forbidden by law), not only revealing Himself to her as THE CHRIST, but also telling her of the GREAT SHIFT about to occur in the way God was to be worshiped — that is, EXTERNAL worship of God **replaced by INTERNAL FELLOWSHIP "in spirit and in truth."** No temple, no mountain, no church building, nothing — wholly INSIDE the believer!

Jesus had never revealed such information to anyone — not even His disciples. This woman's spiritual thirst must have gotten to Him. But did she understand what He was saying? Some of it, perhaps. But the idea of worshiping in "spirit and in truth" to bring God the fellowship He sought, was definitely beyond her. It was beyond the disciples and everyone else — until it actually happened. And you know when that was . . .

AT PENTECOST

Fifty days after the Lord rose from the dead, the disciples, the Lord's brothers and His mother Mary, were gathered with others in an upper room in Jerusalem for prayer. They had been ordered to WAIT for the promised Holy Spirit (Acts 1:4,5,12-14; 2:1).

It was well into the day of Pentecost when suddenly there was a noise . . . a deafening noise. A windblast, generating a sound akin to a SONIC BOOM, thundered down on the room where they were assembled. What was the noise about? It was God supernaturally rapping for attention. He got it, too. The disciples were astonished. They stopped everything, including breathing . . . ready for anything.

Then — suddenly a large FIREBALL appeared over their heads, suspended in mid-air. There was no question what it represented — the presence of God. The disciples knew all about the Shekinah glory that bespoke the presence of God. As children they grew up learning how

God appeared this way in times past.

As they watched open-mouthed, the fireball began to distribute into tongues of flame (Acts 2:2,3). Can you see Peter and the others cringing as the fiery tongues came toward them and settled atop their heads? There was no pain, no singeing, no smoke even. What did it mean? Then, as each one was filled with the Holy Spirit, the meaning became clear. **Just as the fireball had distributed itself, so had Jesus distributed Himself.**

© Linda Lovet 1976

Aflame with the Spirit, Peter may have been the first to remember the Lord's words:

 "At that day ye shall know that I am in My Father, and ye in ME, AND I IN YOU" (John 14:20 KJV).

After all, he'd seen the Lord do a little multiplying with the 5 loaves and 2 fishes to feed 5000 people. Yet here, He was MULTIPLYING HIS PRESENCE, so that everyone could have Him. The action was a dramatic VISUAL AID, explaining an event taking place in the spirit — **the Lord's indwelling presence in each of His disciples.**

THEIR SPIRITS EXPLODED

It was impossible for the disciples to contain their joy and excitement. With Peter in the lead, they rushed from the upper room to broadcast the news of Christ's return in the Spirit. It was just too much to hold. When they got outside, they found the BOOM had attracted a huge crowd, inasmuch as the city was filled with pilgrims celebrating the feast of Pentecost.

As they started to speak, another miracle occurred. When they opened their mouths to speak their native ARAMAIC, the words came off their lips in DIFFERENT LANGUAGES! They were THINKING in one language, yet SPEAKING in another (Acts 2:4)! How could this be?

There was but one explanation . . . and this was the clincher. The Lord was actually INSIDE THEM, manipulating the speech organ. For anyone to be able to do that, it would be necessary for him to KNOW THEIR THOUGHTS and be able to control the SPEECH APPARATUS. It seems they all came to the same conclusion:

the Lord was doing this to convince them He was IN-SIDE THEM. Some three thousand people put their faith in Jesus and received the Spirit (Acts 2:41). From that day on, the way was open to worship the Father in "spirit and in truth."

HOW JESUS MULTIPLIES HIMSELF

You had your own Pentecost!

When you opened your heart to Christ, HE CAME IN! As astonishing as it may sound, there are now **two people** living inside your body — you and the Lord! Via the Holy Spirit, Jesus is as surely a resident of your body as you are. It is for this reason the Bible describes your body as a "temple of the Holy Spirit" (1 Cor. 6:19).

Had Jesus been living in our day, He might have used TELEVISION to explain how He was going to leave His disciples and return IN THE SPIRIT to indwell them. It would have been simple for them to comprehend His indwelling presence.

● Consider how an individual in a TV studio sends his presence to a viewing audience. The studio transmitter radiates his unseen image to the surrounding area. By means of radio waves, he can enter any TV set tuned to his station. Though he is just ONE MAN, he can display himself on every TV screen that tunes him in.

Consider also, how the Lord, in heaven's studio, can reproduce His presence via the Holy Spirit (like radio waves) in every heart that will tune Him in (receive Him). If men can infinitely reproduce their presence in homes by means of circuits and transistors, surely God can bring His **literal presence** into every life that wants Him by means of His Holy Spirit.

CHRIST IN HEAVEN'S STUDIO BROADCASTS HIMSELF IN THE HOLY SPIRIT.

GOD
(Jesus Christ)

Instead of showing **visible** tongues of fire coming to rest on men, I am picturing the Pentecostal diffusion of Christ by showing the **invisible** Spirit coming into men's hearts. This is what the tongues of fire actually represented. Since man is designed as a SPIRIT-RECEIVER, the **forming** of Christ in the believer works almost identically to television (Gal. 4:19).

AS THERE IS NO LIMIT TO THE NUMBER OF SETS THAT CAN TUNE IN A TV STATION, SO IS THERE NO LIMIT TO THE NUMBER OF SOULS THAT CAN RECEIVE CHRIST VIA THE SPIRIT.

Can you see how the Holy Spirit makes Christ available today? In the days of His flesh, Jesus simply was not available. As long as He was locked into a physical body, no one could have Him. You can't stuff one body inside another. Even if such a thing were possible, only one person could be saved by such a method.

There is only ONE Jesus. For Him to be available TO ALL, it was necessary for Him to make the transition from flesh to spirit. **Once He did that, everyone who wanted Him could have all there is of Christ.** This is why the Lord told His disciples He had to leave them. He planned to return and indwell them by means of the Holy Spirit (John 16:7). After that, He'd be as available as television is today.

CHRIST'S PRESENCE — A SOLID FACT

It's easy to read the Word and gloss over truths without realizing how real they are and what they mean to us. Christ's indwelling presence in the believer is not a matter for debate. **It's a settled fact.** Pentecost demonstrated it. The Bible declares it. The Holy Spirit seals it. Personal experience settles it. The New Testament program is based on it. Yet, the only way a believer can enjoy it — is BY FAITH. He has to put his trust in the FACT of the Lord's presence, whether he FEELS it or not.

Feelings or no feelings, **a SPIRIT TO SPIRIT relationship exists when a person opens his heart to Jesus.** Don't you think it's remarkable to have SOMEONE ELSE sharing your body, thoughts, feelings and plans? To

have another person fully intimate with everything going on IN YOUR MIND AND IMAGINATION?

"HEY! I'M NOT AWARE OF ANYONE ELSE SHARING THIS BODY WITH ME!"

Has that thought gone through your head? I wouldn't
blame you if it has. After all, you and I are limited to
the finite senses; taste, touch, smell, seeing and hearing.
Since the Lord is SPIRIT ONLY, we can't behold Him
as we do other people. Nonetheless the Bible INSISTS
Jesus lives inside us whether we're aware of it or not:

"That Christ may dwell in your hearts by faith . . ."
—Eph. 3:17;

and again:

". . . Christ in you, the hope of glory"
— Col. 1:27(KJV).

Inasmuch as the Lord does not have a body, His presence in us is in no way **physical.** The Bible is equally
definite about that:

" . . the last Adam became a life-giving spirit"
—1 Cor. 15:45;

and again:

"Now the Lord is the Spirit . . ."
—2 Cor. 3:17(NAS).

Here's what this means. Right now, you and I have
NO DIRECT contact with Jesus. Though He indwells
us, His presence is beyond our five senses. So how can
we really know Him? **How can we enjoy His presence?
Ah—that is the thrill of faith. Faith can go where reason
cannot follow.** And what is faith? The ability to count
as real, that which cannot be seen. The ability to trust
in a fact, even when you have no physical contact.

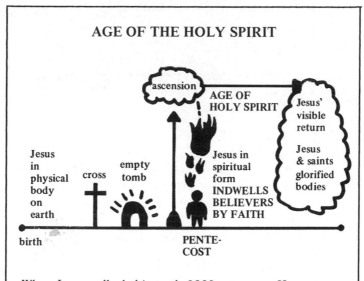

AGE OF THE HOLY SPIRIT

When Jesus walked this earth 2000 years ago, He was worshiped as God's Son, the Messiah (John 6:69). But there was no way for Him to be inside them. During the age of the Holy Spirit, He indwells all believers through the Spirit. But we have to appreciate His presence BY FAITH (2 Cor. 5:16). Even when we pray, we must visualize Him by faith. At His second coming He will again put on a body and "we shall see Him as He is" (1 John 3:2). After that we'll be with Him, never again required to visualize Him by faith.

BUT FAITH CAN BE FUN

It may seem difficult to appreciate Jesus' presence by faith, but it can also be fun. Not in the sense of a game, but in terms of delight when we realize we are participating in an age that will never come again. Only in this age, does Jesus indwell believers. **Only during our lifetime can we use faith to visualize His presence in us.** Once this life is over, faith will be a thing of the past. Some future day, we may look back on the unique privilege that was ours and wish we could relive the experience.

It is an ADVENTURE, too. Here is Jesus . . . IN US . . . but we can't see Him, touch Him or hear Him. Still He enjoys us and asks us to delight in Him (Psa. 37:4). Doesn't that sound like something God invented for our excitement! Indeed. Believe me, it's going to get very exciting as we plunge deeper into the mystery and mechanics of His indwelling, and know the Lord is so CLOSE.

I was in a variety store last week, not far from a mother and her small son. The little fellow was running along the counters, sliding his hand on the glass dividers. He wasn't watching when his mother walked to another part of the store. When he turned around to run back — she was gone!

His panic was instantaneous. "Mama! Mama!" he screamed. I could see the fear in his eyes, the terrified look on his face. His mother heard the cry, "I'm over here, Billy." Ah, that took care of everything. But for a moment he was really scared.

But let me ask, wouldn't you panic if you thought the Lord had shifted His interest from you to other things! That He was so occupied with something else, you were out of His sight! Wow, you'd panic, too.

Praise the Lord, that can't happen. That's the glory of having Him inside us. He's never busy with anything BUT US! And when you learn just where He indwells us, you'll see why Christians need never panic about anything! That's next.

Chapter Four

Where Our Unseen Lord Dwells

"On that day you will realize that I am in My Father, and you are in Me, and I am in you." (John 14:20 NIV)

"The Lord Jesus is waiting at the door of your heart right now. Will you open the door? Will you let Him in?"

I've said those very words to thousands of people. In the earlier years of my ministry, it was a way of life for me to approach people and speak to them of Jesus. I wasn't aware of it at the time, but God was schooling me. In the process of dealing with so many, the Lord brought forth a super plan for winning souls. Putting that plan into print was the beginning of Personal Christianity.*

---

* Many readers will be familiar with **SOUL-WINNING MADE EASY,** the very first book the Lord led me to write. Producing this simple 4-step plan was the beginning point of my literature ministry. Through the years that plan has helped thousands of Christians become skillful soul-winners. It is based on the fact that Jesus is ALIVE and eager to enter any heart that will admit Him. When a person believes that, it changes his entire outlook on winning souls.

The last step in the plan goes like this:

"This is the Lord Jesus speaking to you . . .

 'Behold, I stand at the door, and knock: if any man hear My voice, and open the door, I WILL COME IN . . .' (Rev. 3:20 KJV).

Now that door, dear friend, is the door of your heart. The Lord Jesus wants an invitation to come in. He's too polite to enter without it. He won't force His way into your life. He wants you to invite Him in. Will you open the door? Will you let Him in?"

© Linda Lovett 1978

In the thousands of times I've said those words, I've never had ONE PERSON say to me, "I don't believe He's there!" Not a single soul has ever said, "Man, you're crazy, how can another person possibly come inside me?" Why do you suppose people never give me any static when I tell them Jesus wants to come inside them? You know the answer — the Holy Spirit is vigorously witnessing to their hearts that **Jesus REALLY IS standing at the door waiting to come in.**

COME IN WHERE?

Ah, here is fascination. When we say Jesus is waiting to **come in,** what do we mean? Does He come into our legs? Our arms? Our liver or stomach? That doesn't make sense. He doesn't dwell in our arms or legs or organs any more than we do. Fact is, you can dissect a human body and find NO TRACE of anyone dwelling in it anywhere.

For confirmation, visit a funeral home. Take a good look at a corpse. It's complete, no missing parts. Yet one thing is sure — THE MAN IS GONE! There's only one conclusion: Man is NOT A BODY, he merely wears one, like an earth suit, for as long as he's in the flesh. Still the question remains — when the man was in the body WHERE DID HE DWELL? And when Jesus comes in, where does He dwell? When we learn the answer to that, we will have solved the mystery of man and his body.

THE MYSTERY OF MAN

"Then God said, 'Let us make man in our image and likeness to rule the fish in the sea, the birds of heaven, the cattle, all the wild animals on earth, and all reptiles that crawl upon the earth.'

Then the Lord God formed a man from the dust of the ground and breathed into his nostrils the breath of life. Thus the man became a living creature.

So God created man in His own image; in the image of God He created him; male and female He created them."
— Gen. 1:26, 27; 2:7 NEB

No mystery is more exciting than how God made us and where the Lord indwells us. Even the mechanics are exciting.

God has taken His image and placed it in a human body (creature) thus creating a **man** (woman). Equipped with an actual body, the image (which is spirit) can get around on the earth. There's no way to live on this earth without a body. As an astronaut needs a space suit and a diver needs a wet suit, so does God's image need an "earth suit." Let's consider the two amazing entities that COMBINE to make a man.

FIRST: we have the image of God. He's just like God, an infinite, spirit-being. HE can THINK and CREATE and ENJOY EXISTENCE in spirit form totally independent of any body. He is in essence a THINKING MIND. No matter what FORM he might occupy, his MIND functions by itself. The mind does not require a body of any kind in order to THINK.

SECOND: we have a body God designed for His image. It's perfectly suited for what God has in mind. It's earth-bound, that is it would CONFINE His image to a two-legged creature living on the earth. The two-legged creature, which scientists refer to as "homo sapiens," belongs to the animal kingdom. But that doesn't matter, for it has a brain which is fed by the five senses of the body.

The brain, you see, is capable of **processing thoughts**. Observe, I didn't say it could think. But since it can process thoughts, that means it can also be used for THINKING. A brain can't think by itself any more than a computer can think by itself. Someone has to use it. SOMEONE HAS TO THINK WITH IT. That's the key. The human brain is perfect for someone who can think — A THINKING MIND.

Who is a thinking mind? Certainly not animals. It is YOU. You are God's image and therefore a thinking mind.

> **ANIMALS CAN'T THINK.** While all animals have brains, not one uses it for thinking. Animals operate entirely by instinct. Their brains are used merely to execute their instinctual behavior. They are programmed. This is why fish already know how to swim, spiders weave webs and bees know how to sting. No matter how creative they APPEAR in these things, it is all done by instinct alone.

Here's what God has done with us. **He has joined His image (a thinking MIND) to the BRAIN of a living creature (human form), and He called the combination — MAN!** At once His image becomes a prisoner of both the body and the brain of the creature. Even so, he can USE IT as though it were his own. So when he looks in the mirror and sees his face, he says, "It is my face!"

STUCK IN A BRAIN

Here we are . . . God's image . . . THINKING MINDS, capable of thinking as God thinks, yet imprisoned in a BRAIN and limited to the physical awareness of the creature serving as our earth suit. Bound in this finite state, we're cut off from immediate AWARENESS OF GOD, for we only know what the brain knows. It is being a prisoner of the brain that makes the faith method possible.

IMAGE OF GOD (MIND) AND HIS BODY JOINED AT THE BRAIN

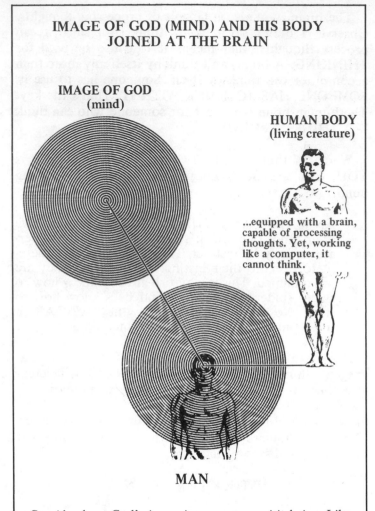

IMAGE OF GOD
(mind)

HUMAN BODY
(living creature)

...equipped with a brain, capable of processing thoughts. Yet, working like a computer, it cannot think.

MAN

Consider how God's image is an unseen, spirit being. Like God, he's a THINKING MIND, with nothing physical about him. Now look at the human body with its BRAIN. It is totally physical, with nothing spiritual about it. How can these completely opposites be joined? At what point are they compatible? If they are to be wedded somehow, just where would the union occur? The answer: in the BRAIN.

If you and I were not limited to the brains that come with our bodies, we'd be aware of all that goes on in the spirit world. But our limitation is God's ingenious way of separating us from our NATURAL HABITAT (heaven) and putting the **faith program** into operation. **Faith would not be possible if we had access to the spirit world.**

We've just made a whopping discovery!

We now know how God isolates us from the spirit world. He LIMITS our thinking to the creature's brain. In that way we only know what comes to the brain by way of the body's 5 senses. It's a temporary situation, of course, for when the body dies and the brain ceases to function, its hold on us is broken. Death releases us from our mental prisons. We will then be thinking at the MIND LEVEL. Obvously, that's what God intended from the beginning. So keep this fact before you . . .

WHILE THE BODY IS EQUIPPED WITH A BRAIN, THE IMAGE OF GOD IS A MIND. THE MIND AND THE BRAIN ARE TWO SEPARATE ENTITIES.

WHERE THE MIND JOINS THE BRAIN

A glance at the drawing on the next page quickly defines the difference between the MIND and the BRAIN. You can even see the very point at which the two meet. Note how the MIND (God's image) has its center in the CONSCIOUS. **The faith method depends on clear-cut separation between our two kinds of mental experience — conscious and unconscious.**

● Consider an iceberg. The human MIND is like that. Icebergs are deceiving. Only 10% of their bulk is above water. The rest sprawls beneath the surface. The part above the water line we call the CONSCIOUS. The

71

greater part lying below the surface we call the UNCON-SCIOUS or subconscious. In this book I will be using the term UNCONSCIOUS when referring to that part of our mental history which is out of sight, or BEYOND AWARENESS.

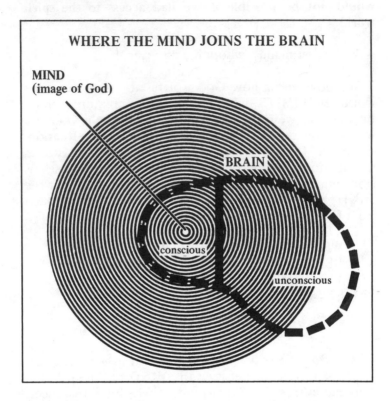

WHERE THE MIND JOINS THE BRAIN

MIND
(image of God)

BRAIN

conscious

unconscious

The CONSCIOUS is where we live. This is that part of our mental activity where we have AWARENESS. This is where we THINK, FEEL THINGS, IMAGINE AND MAKE DECISIONS. We experience life in the conscious mind. That is, you are aware that you are sitting and reading. A book is in your hand. You're aware of the chair, the room, everything about you . . . what day it is and what your plans are. The conscious is the LIVING-ROOM of life.

The **UNCONSCIOUS is that part of your mental history that lies BEYOND AWARENESS.** 90% of your lifetime experiences lie in the unconscious, because they have slipped from memory and are stored in the unconscious.

Like the memory banks of a computer, your unconscious holds every thought you've ever had, every feeling you've ever felt, every good or bad time you've ever known throughout your life. **Also your unconscious is in touch with God.** Any influence He wishes to exert upon your thoughts or actions, He does through your unconscious. Another name you can give your unconscious is **your spirit.** When God ministers to you through your unconscious or spirit, we call it **inspiration**-spirit to spirit (Rom. 8:16).

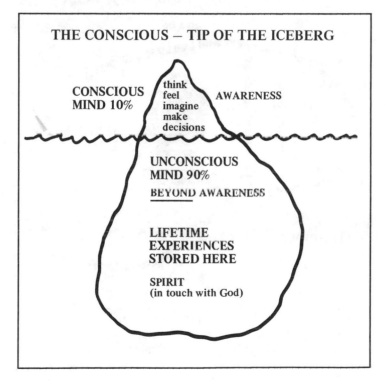

THE CONSCIOUS – TIP OF THE ICEBERG

CONSCIOUS MIND 10%

think
feel
imagine
make
decisions

AWARENESS

UNCONSCIOUS MIND 90%

BEYOND AWARENESS

LIFETIME EXPERIENCES STORED HERE

SPIRIT
(in touch with God)

JESUS' HOME IN US

Now we're ready to consider the question of where Jesus dwells. The answer is easy now. **When we invite Christ into our lives, He takes up residence in the UN-CONSCIOUS.** You could tell me why — because it is BEYOND AWARENESS. Were He to join us at the CONSCIOUS LEVEL, we'd be aware of His immediate presence and faith would not be needed. Such a thing would wipe out the faith method. By establishing Himself in the UNCONSCIOUS area of our being, He can share in every bit of our mental activity without any DIRECT CONTACT at all. Isn't that ingenious! Here is how it works:

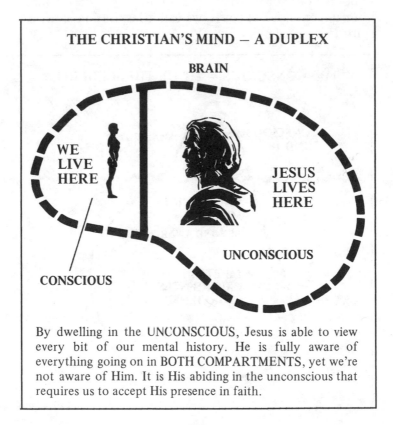

THE CHRISTIAN'S MIND — A DUPLEX

BRAIN

WE LIVE HERE

JESUS LIVES HERE

UNCONSCIOUS

CONSCIOUS

By dwelling in the UNCONSCIOUS, Jesus is able to view every bit of our mental history. He is fully aware of everything going on in BOTH COMPARTMENTS, yet we're not aware of Him. It is His abiding in the unconscious that requires us to accept His presence in faith.

As you look at the drawing, do you get the feeling the Christian's mind is like a DUPLEX? The believer living on one side, the Lord on the other? Well, that's just what it is — A DUPLEX. There are two people dwelling in the creature (your body); however, one of them (Jesus) has to abide in the UNCONSCIOUS so as not to upset the faith program. But Jesus doesn't mind. He likes it there. He's as close to you as He always wanted to be, yet the faith method is not violated.

HOW WE VIEW JESUS

Not long ago I saw an episode of "Starsky & Hutch", a TV police series. Starsky had brought in a suspect for questioning, purposely taking him to an interrogation room equipped with a two-way mirror. You know what those are. On one side, you see only yourself. It's a real mirror. However the other side is like a window. You can look through it to see what's going on, yet those on the other side can't see you.

So as not to blow his cover, Hutch stayed on the window side watching Starsky fire questions at the suspect. He watched every move, taking careful note of the suspect's actions and words. At the same time, he knew he couldn't be seen. This allowed Hutch to watch the suspect betray himself, even as he denied Starsky's allegations.

● Why do I tell that story? Only to draw attention to the TWO-WAY MIRROR. You see, we have such a mirror in our minds. Look again at the BOLD LINE separating the conscious from the unconscious. Well, that's not just a line. **It's a two-way mirror. You and I live on the mirror side. Jesus dwells on the window side. While we can't see Him, He beholds us perfectly.**

We can't, of course, but suppose we could go around to the BACK SIDE of the mirror for a look. What would we find? No mirror on that side, but a window. We would be able to see what Jesus sees — a clear view into our thought life, right into our CONSCIOUS. That's why He can see us as we are.

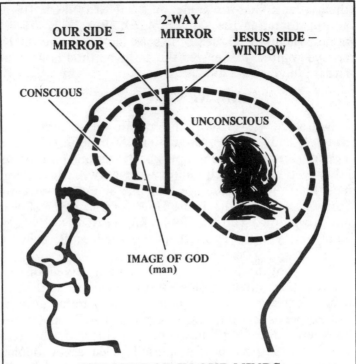

THE MIRROR IN OUR MINDS

Observe the image of God in the conscious. I now show Him in human form looking at the mirror. What does he see? His own reflection. He sees himself, but not too well. Not all the information about himself is visible. Most of it is stored in the unconscious. Very little of it is actually present in the conscious. This is why the apostle Paul says, "we see through a glass (mirror), darkly." There's a lot you don't know about yourself now. But one day you will know, "even as also I am known" (1 Cor. 13:12). Thus Jesus knows you better than you know yourself, for He has information from BOTH SIDES of the mirror.

So how do we **lay hold** of Jesus? By using . . .

THE IMAGINATION SCREEN

Take another look at the bold dividing line separating the conscious from the unconscious. This time consider it as **MORE THAN A 2-WAY MIRROR.** It is also a kind of television screen. Not only do we see ourselves reflected there, but also our thinking. In fact, this is where we do our thinking — on that screen. We all think in pictures. **So we now have another name for the mirror — THE IMAGINATION SCREEN.**

When we imagine, we project pictures on that SCREEN. We take whatever we wish from the data available to us and FORM PICTURES on this screen of the mind. Animals use this screen to SEE WITH. We use it to THINK WITH.* **Since it is an IMAGINATION SCREEN, we can use this screen to VISUALIZE Jesus' presence in us.** We can project an IMAGE OF JESUS onto this screen, and it is an authentic act, because He is just on the other side of that screen anyway.

HOW JESUS BEHOLDS US

Don't you find it exciting to realize how CLOSE Jesus is to us . . . just on the other side of the MIRROR/IMAGINATION SCREEN, in the unconscious. What a glorious mystery. What precious knowledge. With the Lord dwelling in the unconscious portion of our mental activity, nothing is hidden from His eye.

 ". . . **all things are naked and opened unto the eyes of Him with Whom we have to do**" (Heb. 4:13 KJV).

---

* Interested in the technical aspects of the mind and the imagination screen, as well as how to use it for weight reduction and healing? See the author's books: **JESUS WANTS YOU WELL** and **"HELP LORD — THE DEVIL WANTS ME FAT!"**

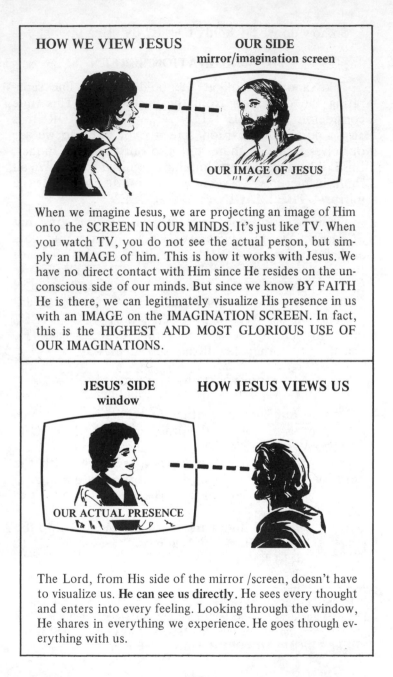

HOW WE VIEW JESUS

OUR SIDE
mirror/imagination screen

OUR IMAGE OF JESUS

When we imagine Jesus, we are projecting an image of Him onto the SCREEN IN OUR MINDS. It's just like TV. When you watch TV, you do not see the actual person, but simply an IMAGE of him. This is how it works with Jesus. We have no direct contact with Him since He resides on the unconscious side of our minds. But since we know BY FAITH He is there, we can legitimately visualize His presence in us with an IMAGE on the IMAGINATION SCREEN. In fact, this is the HIGHEST AND MOST GLORIOUS USE OF OUR IMAGINATIONS.

JESUS' SIDE
window

HOW JESUS VIEWS US

OUR ACTUAL PRESENCE

The Lord, from His side of the mirror /screen, doesn't have to visualize us. **He can see us directly**. He sees every thought and enters into every feeling. Looking through the window, He shares in everything we experience. He goes through everything with us.

Familiar with **both sides** of our thought life, He can distinguish between the "thoughts and intents of the heart" (Heb. 4:12b). He knows us through and through.

Does it bother you to realize that Jesus watches everything taking place in your head; that He sees everything going on in your imagination? It could — until you also realize He isn't there to JUDGE you, but to **help** you. He accepts you just as you are, faults and all . . . and still thinks you're fabulous. No way does His presence threaten us. Actually, it's a relief to realize **He sees the WORST in us and loves us still.** Inspite of all the terrible stuff He beholds, He wants us desparately. Hallelujah!

What joy and peace it brings to the believer to realize he's totally acceptable to Jesus; that the Lord lives to HELP him grow up in His likeness, **and there is "no condemnation" of any kind** (Rom. 8:1).

THROUGH THE LOOKING GLASS — BY FAITH

Let's flash back to the interrogation scene with Starsky and Hutch. Though the suspect had been questioned at length, he wouldn't admit to a thing. Very frustrating for the detective duo, for everything about his movements and expressions indicated he was guilty. With a shrug of exasperation Starsky mumbled, "You can go. Go on, get out of here!"

The suspect rose from his chair, but didn't go directly to the door. Very pleased with himself, he strode belligerently to the two-way mirror, waved his hand and said, "Hi Hutch, I know you're back there." Then, chuckling aloud, he went out the door.

Somewhat startled by this move, Hutch was caught off guard. He jumped back from the mirror. In a flash he realized he couldn't be seen. It left him a bit embarrased at his own reaction.

The suspect, you see, had been questioned in this room before. He knew about the two-way mirror. He also knew Starsky and Hutch worked as a team, so he assumed, BY FAITH, the unseen partner was behind the glass. It was by faith he spoke to Hutch and waved to him, **even though he couldn't see him**. And his faith was on good ground. Hutch was there.

IT'S LIKE THAT FOR US

Naturally our relationship is not that of a police officer and suspect. **Our relationship is that of Father and son.** Therefore we would approach the MENTAL MIRROR very differently, and our actions and words would be different, too.

In our next chapters I'll show you how to boldly approach the two-way mirror and speak tenderly to the Lord. When it finally dawns on you how close He is and how He aches for your fellowship, you may be surprised at the words coming from your mouth. We'll see.

Chapter Five

The
"Secret Place"

"He that dwelleth in the secret place of the Most High
shall abide under the shadow of the Almighty."
(Psalm 91:1 KJV)

When I was a little fellow, my favorite place was Grandpa's lap. He'd sit in his big rocker and I'd climb up and snuggle next to him. To me, there was no safer place. I was fond of Grandpa. At times I'd say, "Grandpa, I sure love you. You're the best grandpa in the whole world." Satisfaction would shiver through him when I said that. I could feel it.

Grandpa's death left a crater in my soul. I missed that lap, that place of safety. The ache didn't go away until I was born again and got to know my Heavenly Father. Now I crawl up in His lap and tell Him the same thing.

This may sound silly to you, but when I'm with God in the "secret place," I often put my arms around Him and say, "Father I love you. You're the greatest Dad anyone could have." Sometimes I'm emotional as I shower my affection on Him. Then I sense that same SHIVER OF SATISFACTION go through Him I felt in Grandpa. It delights Him to have me give Him a big hug and tell Him I love Him.

THE "SECRET PLACE"

Every Christian has a "secret place," whether he is aware of it or not. There is a room in your imagination where you meet the Lord. Notice how people close their eyes to pray? Know why they do this? It's not simply to shut out their surroundings; they're using their imaginations to picture the Lord. They think of themselves as talking to Him. Where? In the "secret place."

David knew of this place. The Psalmist of Israel spent a lot of time there. Thus he could affirm,

"He that dwelleth in the SECRET PLACE of the Most High shall abide under the shadow of the Almighty" (Psa. 91:1 KJV).

You should start thinking about this room. **It's the most important place in your life.**

WHERE IS IT, EXACTLY?

The "secret place" is YOUR SIDE of the imagination screen. This is the ROOM where you meet with Jesus.

When we visualize Jesus on the screen of our minds, we are at once in the "secret place." We're in His presence. We see ourselves with Him — on that screen. Look what we have done! **BY FAITH, we have brought the Lord from the unconscious side, over to our side.** Isn't that amazing! Can we do that? Yes. We've already defined faith as the ability to ACCEPT the unseen as real, and imagination as the ability to PICTURE the unseen reality. This is why we say, "faith can go where reason cannot follow."

YOUR SIDE
of imagination screen

THE "SECRET PLACE"

We have already spoken of the IMAGINATION SCREEN. It is the same mirror-like divider that makes a duplex of our minds, allowing the Lord to dwell on one side and we the other. It works like a TV screen. We put the picture on it ourselves during our conscious hours. At night, pictures can come from the other side in the form of dreams. No matter how the pictures originate, we see them on this screen. It's called the imagination screen, because we do all of our visualizing on it.

Even though we have no direct contact with the Lord, via our imaginations we can bring Him to our side and enjoy Him. The process looks something like this:

BRINGING THE LORD TO OUR SIDE — BY FAITH

THE "SECRET PLACE"
imagination screen

JESUS IS
REALLY
HERE

YOU
VISUALIZE
HIM HERE

While the Lord continues to remain on the unconscious side of the screen, nonetheless we can BRING HIM by faith over to our side by visualizing Him on the IMAGINATION SCREEN. When we do, OUR SIDE becomes the "SECRET PLACE."

IMAGINATION

We come now to what is likely our most fantastic ability, one that sets us apart from the animals and makes us completely unique — **the ability to IMAGINE.** By means of our imaginations we can SEE THINGS that do not exist. Before a man can build a bridge, must he not SEE IT in his mind? Did not someone have to visualize a television set before one could be made? Surely, flights to the moon were pictured in men's minds before anyone was sent there.

Imagination is the key to creation. Everything God is doing He first sees in His mind. And so it is with men made in His image. While men use their imaginations to create and invent (hardly surprising since they're made in the image of the Creator), this is not its highest purpose.

THE MOST NOBLE AND GLORIOUS PURPOSE OF THE IMAGINATION IS GIVING REALITY TO THE UNSEEN LORD!

You and I accept what the Word says about Jesus' indwelling. Yet we can't see Him, touch Him or contact Him, can we? Even so, we know BY FAITH He lives within us. While our faith allows us to accept what we can't see, we don't stop there. **Imagination takes us a step beyond, allowing us to PICTURE what we cannot see.** Isn't that remarkable! Therefore visualizing our indwelling Lord and Lover is the most thrilling and exciting use of our imaginations!

DUAL PURPOSE. Like everything else, our imaginations can be used two ways: to please God or the devil. Satan loves to have us create scenes in our minds that don't exist. This is how we worry, you know, by visualizing things that MIGHT GO WRONG. Without imagination, worry would be impossible. Beyond that, Satan prods (tempts) us to create carnal scenes (lust, envy, pride, etc.) perverting the use of the imagination, something that gives him fiendish pleasure. Consequently we have to WORK at keeping the Lord before us in our imaginations, for this is the best way to frustrate the work of the devil.*

---

* For more information on resisting Satan's luring temptations, refer to the author's book **DEALING WITH THE DEVIL**. It offers a 4-step plan for putting him to flight.

KEEPING THE "SECRET PLACE" SECRET

Visit your lawyer in a downtown building and one of his doors will be marked "PRIVATE." That's his own entrance to his office. Visitors must enter by way of the receptionist's desk. In that way he guards his privacy. Similarly, **the "secret place" is the most private place you own. Only two people belong there — you and Jesus.**

In this very private place, you and the Lord share your innermost thoughts, hopes and desires. **It is here that you worship Him in spirit, making it the holiest place in your life.** The more time you spend here with Him, the more you become like Him. You've noticed how husbands and wives become very much alike with the passing of years. Well the same can be true of you and the Lord.

You may wish to give a name to the "secret place." I have. I call mine the "rendezvous room!" It adds a dash of romance, making it even more real to me. What I like is the TOTAL PRIVACY. What goes on here is known only to Jesus and me. When we meet in this room, I can be myself. I can say anything to the Lord and know it will go no further. Absolutely secret.

Here's how it works for me. I've trained myself to enter the "rendezvous room" . . . shut the door . . . and leave the world outside. All it takes is a bit of practice. Anyone can do it. And it can be done any place. Should I be in a crowded doctor's office for example, I can turn off the DIN of my surroundings by slipping into the "secret place" for a chat with the Lord. It's as though we were alone in the middle of a desert. A very nice feature in view of the hustle and bustle of today's fast pace.

"FIXIN UP" THE ROOM

Here's some fun for your imagination.

Do you like to pick out room furnishings? Good. Then you can design the "rendezvous room" any way you like. I mean you can imagine it to look like a den, if you wish . . . paneling, fireplace, thick carpet, deeply stuffed chairs, etc.

Still others might prefer the room to have a sanctuary character, reminding them of church. If that helps to make it more real, fine. A woman, on the other hand, might visualize it like a sunny porch with lots of plants. Maybe a library. A mountain cabin, or a Galillean seaside resort. It can be anything . . . as long as it is a comfortable place for you and the Lord to spend time together. The more attractive it is to you, the more you'll be inclined to spend time alone with Jesus.

It bears repeating — the beauty of this room is its isolation from the outside world. You can slip into it in a flash. Even if you're standing in line at a bank or post office, regretting the waste of time, you can convert that same time into spiritual gold by transporting yourself (in the spirit) into the "rendezvous room." I guarantee it won't bother you a bit if the line moves slowly. For the moment, you'll be LIVING ABOVE YOUR CIRCUMSTANCES, making your time count with Jesus.

VISUALIZING JESUS

This, of course, is what we're really after.

Once you've prepared the "rendezvous room," fixing it up to your delight, **it is time to work on visualizing the Lord.** The room and its "fixins" are secondary, meant only to help you visualize Jesus. Thus we come to the place where I can be of real help.

As you know, many tend to be superstitious about picturing the Lord. That is, they tend to regard Him as too holy or too glorious to be reduced to a form in our minds. **But you see, the Lord doesn't care ONE BIT how we visualize Him.** He's neither pompous nor pious. Anyone willing to humble Himself on a cross for us isn't going to fuss over the way we picture Him in our minds. Besides, if it were necessary to have a specific image, He'd give us one.

> **FUSS.** While the Lord isn't fussy about our image of Him, some Christians might be. Not only will they object to picturing Him in any form, they also object to paying so much attention to Him. They feel it should go to the Father rather than the Son. I won't be able to satisfy everyone on this matter, but when you come right down to it, JESUS IS THE ONLY GOD WE KNOW. No man has seen the Father. But the Lord made it very clear that anyone seeing Him, had also seen the Father (John 14: 9). And as far as giving undue honor to Jesus, we've been instructed to HONOR THE SON EVEN AS WE HONOR THE FATHER (John 5:23). So we're not in trouble by giving such attention to Jesus.

How do you normally think of Jesus? A vague, shadowy presence floating about? There's nothing wrong with that — **as long as His presence is REAL to you.** However, we're fleshly individuals. We think of people in terms of faces, arms and legs. We like to touch. A person is real to us when we can shake hands with him and give him a hug.

THE FACE OF JESUS

Above my typewriter hangs my favorite oil painting. It is my daughter's painting of Jesus, **"Alone With Him."** Linda works closely with me in the ministry. This particular painting reminds me to slip into the "secret place" when I run into writing problems. If I get stuck (and I often do), I shut my eyes momentarily and there is Jesus . . . waiting for me in our "rendezvous room." He's all set to chat with me about the problem. Moments later, my eyes open and the typewriter is clacking again.

Here's the painting as it hangs on the wall in front of me, just slightly above my line of vision. Maybe now you can guess the image I have of Jesus when I'm "alone with Him."

No one on earth knows, of course, what Jesus really looked like in human form. This is simply Linda's conception of Him. I like it because of the superb blending of gentleness with strength. It helps me to think of Jesus as strong enough to discipline me when I need it, yet understanding enough to sympathize with my weakness. Yes, it influences my concept of Jesus. I just love it.

FACE. I'm not saying I give Jesus a face EXACT-
LY like Linda's painting. Only that it powerfully
influences my visualization of Him. Then, a little
of Grandpa creeps in, too. The things I cherished
in Grandpa sort of automatically show up in Jesus.
The same will be true of you. You're going to be
influenced by pictures you've seen. Many tell me,
for example, Sallman's **"Head of Christ"** dramatically shapes their concept of the Lord. Endearing
things about a friend of the past might find their
way into your portrayal of Him. **As long as we DO
NOT worship the image, but simply use it to give
reality to our unseen Lord, He is pleased with our
effort.**

I'm sure I speak with the Spirit when I say Jesus
doesn't care what face or body you give Him in the "secret place." It's your coming to Him that thrills Him.
**Picture Him any way you wish, but love Him. Enjoy
Him. Delight in Him.** I know from experience, your en-
joyment of Him is going to be greatly enhanced by giving Him arms with which to hold you.*

ENTERING THE "RENDEZVOUS ROOM"

Now that our room is all fixed up and an image of
Jesus rests comfortably with your spirit, **it's time to put
the images together on the imagination screen.** So now
. . . relax. I mean, take a deep breath. Let it out and
close your eyes for just a moment. Relaxation is important. Tension, the opposite of relaxation, is the enemy
of the imagination. The more relaxed you are, the better
your imagination will work.

★ **All right, picture the room.**

---

* Full color reproductions of Linda's paintings including **"Alone
With Him"** are available from Personal Christianity. These can
help you visualize the Lord in the "secret place." Send for free
brochure.

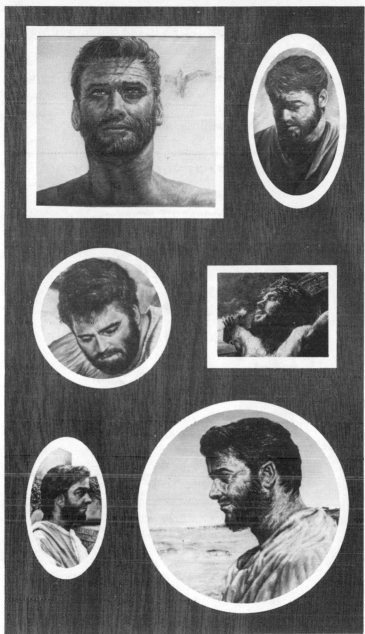

Picture Jesus any way you wish, but love Him, enjoy Him, delight in Him.

★ Now picture the Lord. He's in the room, waiting for you.

★ By faith, walk into the room. It's familiar to you. So is He.

★ There He is. He's smiling, glad to see you.

ENTERING THE "RENDEZVOUS ROOM"

the "secret place"/imagination screen

JESUS' PRESENCE BY FAITH

Go ahead . . . walk right into the Lord's presence. Take Heb. 4:16 on faith and "come boldly" into His presence.

DRAWING NIGH TO OUR LORD

How do you like the idea of being in the SAME ROOM with Jesus . . . by faith? Sound scary? It might, especially if this is new to you. Yet, there's nothing to fear. The Lord ACHES to have us "draw nigh" to Him in the "secret place." This is what he died for — fellowship with those who love Him. So . . .

"Draw nigh to God, and He will draw nigh to you . . ." (James 4:8 KJV).

You've read that verse lots of times, and probably thought it was a salvation invitation. No, those words are **not** for the lost. **It's an invitation to believers to draw close to Christ.** On the surface, it's very plain — **the closer we get to Him, the closer He'll be to us.** Apparently, we can cuddle as close as our faith will take us. It's time for me to say once more, "Faith can go where reason cannot follow."

COME AS YOU ARE

"Why I wouldn't dare go into Jesus' presence! I'm too dirty, too sinful! He wouldn't be glad to see someone like me!"

If that thought passes through your head, forget it. One thing about Jesus, He doesn't expect you to dress up before you can draw close to Him. **He wants you to come . . . JUST AS YOU ARE.** That means overalls, workclothes or whatever you're wearing as you plow your way through this sin-cursed world, for . . .

 " . . . God sees not as man sees, for man looks at the outward appearance, but the Lord looks at the heart" (1 Sam. 16:7 NAS).

And don't worry about formality, either. Jesus doesn't stand on ceremony. Men love ceremony, because it makes their importance stand out. But Jesus isn't like that. There's absolutely no protocol to be learned. We don't have to bow or curtsy or be afraid of doing or saying the wrong thing. Just ENJOY HIM . . . and that's it!

PROTOCOL. If you had an appointment with the queen of England, you'd have to learn how to conduct yourself in her presence. There would be rules to follow, customs to observe. Someone would have to coach you in all that would be expected of you. It's always that way with man. He loves the showy stuff. You know — ego. But with the RULER OF THE UNIVERSE, it's not like that. There's nothing stuffy about Him, nothing pretentious. So, THERE ARE NO RULES. Having laid aside the majesty of heaven to die for us, He's not about to impose a barrier now. He'd rather have us come . . . JUST AS WE ARE, . . . for we are more precious to Him than all the wealth of heaven.

When it dawns on us WHO WE ARE and the RIGHTEOUSNESS we have in Christ, we can go into the presence of God, slam the door and say, "Hi Dad" — if we wish. Kids do that. We're His kids. Children don't have to be cautious when entering the presence of their parents. They just go in, plop in a comfortable chair and start talking about anything that interests them.

PLOP. To understand the casualness I have in mind, picture youngsters in their own home. They're totally at ease. We're the "children of God" (1st John 3:2). It doesn't disturb God one bit to have us enter the "secret place" and plop in His presence. Depending on the mood I'm in, I come to God in different ways. Sometimes I'm casual, other times I'm urgent. If I'm in trouble, it's the latter. Then I rush into His arms. At other times, I just like to crawl up in His lap and feel the safety of those "everlasting arms." Still, there are times when both of us (the Lord and I) prop our feet on the coffee table and chat away. This is why I easily find in Him everything I longed for in a father. Please note, however, it is my visualization of Him that makes it all possible.

THE POINT — BE YOURSELF

This is the thrust of what I'm saying — BE YOURSELF in the Lord's presence. After all, you're with your

BEST FRIEND. Since He knows you better than you know yourself, there's no need to PRETEND anything. Just relax — let Him love you JUST AS YOU ARE. There isn't anything you have to hide or can't discuss with Him. He's seen and heard everything. Even if your sins are offensive to Him, He approves of you **personally**. There's absolutely no reason to feel threatened in His presence. All He cares about is **you**.

All this may require some adjustment on your part. It's no small thing to have the eternal God for your "BOSOM BUDDY." On the surface, the idea seems unbelievable. Consequently it takes a bit of adjusting to get used to intimacy with the Almighty. Yet this is precisely what HE wants, what He died to obtain.

THE FROSTING ON THE CAKE

Does what I've said so far make you eager to start enjoying Him in the "secret place?" Of course. We'll be doing that in a moment. But first I want you to know what this will do for you. If you can lay hold of this, you will give FRIENDSHIP WITH JESUS the priority in your life. Here's the payoff:

> ONCE YOU GET ACCUSTOMED TO ENJOYING THE LORD IN THE "SECRET PLACE," YOU WILL KNOW HIM SO WELL THAT WHEN YOU MEET HIM IN THE AIR ON THAT GLORIOUS DAY, THERE WILL BE NO THREAT AT ALL. IN FACT, THE TRANSITION WILL HARDLY BE NOTICED.

> You'll find yourself saying, "Hi, Lord Jesus! Wow, do You look fantastic! I knew this was going to be exciting, but it sure surpasses anything I imagined! Man, it's great being here with You!"

Do you see what I'm talking about? You know the Lord so intimately, so casually, that you're not stunned or overawed when you join Him in the sky! It's just the CONTINUATION of a glorious friendship you cultivated in the flesh. This releases you to rejoice with your dear Friend.You're delighted for Him. You're proud to see every knee bowed before Him as "King of Kings" and "Lord of Lords" (Phil. 2:9-11).

Yet — there's no fear. No threat. You've already established your INTIMACY with Him, and you're not intimidated by the majesty of His Person. This is your "Bosom Buddy," the One you've enjoyed for so long in the "secret place." Though your relationship is close, your knee bows too. It's a joy to worship Someone so wonderful, so exciting!

WHERE DO WE GO FROM HERE?

We've covered precious ground. For some, I guess, the book could end right here and their souls would be satisfied. But we've just started. **Part Two** beckons us to the "secret place." Yes, that's where we're headed. You and I are going to go in together. I want to be with you to make sure you gain everything possible from the experience, and get to know the Lord as I do.

It's important that you get off to a good start. That's why I'm coming along. You might be tempted to back away from DRAWING CLOSE to the eternal God, believing it to be too scary. But if I'm with you, you'll find plenty of courage in His presence. Afterwards, when you see how eager the Lord was for you to come to Him in this way, you'll be glad I didn't let you shrink back.

You'll see. Next.

A SPECIAL WORD

Are you widowed? Live alone? Shut in?
Been disappointed by a close friend or mate?
Maybe you've never had a real sweetheart, or
mother or father who truly loved you and
showed it. If that's your situation, stay with
me. Don't be afraid to follow me all the way.
This can be the answer to your deepest longing. **Believe me, what I'm about to share with
you – enjoying Jesus in the secret place – is
the perfect answer for a lonely heart.** You
need never suffer that pain again. I know. I've
been there.

Practical Section- "Doing It!"

In this section you will meet THREE LEVELS of delighting in the Lord. These are not just steps for reading — you'll actually BE DOING THEM.

I'd like to caution you not to be in a hurry in doing these steps. Purpose to stay on each level until you are comfortable. The Lord wants us to be fully at ease in His presence, and the only way to develop this ease is to learn to be comfortable with Him at the lower level before moving to the next higher one. This is the way to get the most out of this book.

Chapter Six

ʟevel One-
Getting To
ᴋnow ʏou

"Familiarity leads to intimacy."

*Becoming familiar with the Lord is the **first step**
to intimate fellowship. At this level, we will become
skilled in visualizing the Lord and enjoying His
presence — BY FAITH. While this will be new to
some, it is easily learned. You'll find this simple plan
eases you into the Lord's presence on a day-by-day basis.*

---

*"Getting to know you,
   getting to know all about you.
Getting to like you,
   getting to like everything you do.*

*Getting to love
   all the beautiful and new
   things I'm learning about you
   day by day."*

Recognize those words? They're from *"The King And I."* This delightful lyric nicely expresses what this chapter is all about. The more you know about a friend, the sweeter the fellowship.

It takes time to know someone intimately. You've got to be together a lot. Family members, sharing the same house, get to know each other very intimately, for they become involved with each other's problems as well as their affections.

Knowing Jesus as an intimate, personal friend takes that kind of sharing. We've got to be in touch with Him hour after hour, learning more and more about Him. When we do, we find Him to be a fabulous, exciting companion in good times and bad. Without argument ...

TO KNOW JESUS IS TO LOVE HIM.

That's what we're going to be doing in this chapter, getting in touch with Jesus. By that I mean, we're going to go directly into His presence. Now if the thought of being IN TOUCH with God frightens you — RELAX! We'll be doing this together. Yes, I'm going to be with you each step of the way. In step by step fashion, I'm going to show you how easy it is to make contact with Him. I had an experience in World War II that makes me realize how important it is for me to be with you as we do this the first time.

SOMEONE HELPED ME

I was a W. W. II pilot. First I served as a multi-engine instructor for some years, then I was sent overseas to India. There, my initial assignment was that of operations officer at the New Delhi airport.

Captain Ron Bass lived in the basha (living quarters) next to mine, and it was natural that we would become friends. Ron had a swell job, personal pilot to Commanding General Terry of the China-Burma-India theater of war. It was easy to see why the general liked Ron. He was a tall, lanky fellow. Real macho. Very professional. I liked him, too.

Before long, I was invited to accompany Ron on cross-country flights in the general's elegantly furnished DC-3. I served as his co-pilot. After a number of flights, Ron's tour of duty was finished and it was time for him to return to the states. But first he was given the responsibility of finding a replacement pilot for the general. When he asked me if I'd be interested, I jumped at the chance. Arrangements were then made for me to be interviewed by General Terry.

"I'll take you in myself," offered Ron. **"I'll introduce you to the general and tell him about the times we've flown together and give you my personal endorsement."**

"Boy, I'm glad you're going with me, Ron. I'd be plenty nervous with a general quizzing me. I don't even know how to act in the presence of a general."

"All you have to do," shrugged Ron, **"is be yourself. Generals are no different from anyone else."**

That was easy for him to say. He'd been there. Yet he was determined to set me at ease. He didn't want me so uptight I'd blow the interview. I guess that's why he offered to go with me and make the introduction. Even so, I wasn't all that relaxed. I knew a threatening moment was ahead. I could feel the pressure mounting.

We arrived at the headquarters building a few minutes early. It was an impressive place, built by the British. It looked more like a palace than a military establishment. The floors were marble — and cold. The atmosphere was

101

so formal, the echo of our shoes seemed out of place. I felt like tiptoeing. A sober-faced aide, complete with white gloves and a glistening steel helmet met us. "I'll bet he spent all morning polishing that thing," I mused.

The aide didn't smile once as he ushered us to a waiting room outside the general's office. Ron had often been here, so it was old stuff to him. But it was different for me. "Whew," I thought, "if that aide is an indication this has to be a 'spit and polish' general." The fellow didn't say one word, just motioned for us to sit down. That only added to my nervousness.

In a moment the stoney-faced aide opened the door and beckoned us to enter. I took a deep breath . . . exhaled . . . "Here we go."

A smile of recognition appeared on the general's face when he saw Ron. He extended his hand. Ron grabbed it, acting very much at home. When the general turned his smile in my direction, it helped some.

"Is this your replacement, Captain Bass?"

"Yes, general, I'd like you to meet Captain Lovett."

The general reached out his hand to me. I think I was half-bowing as we exchanged greetings. In a few minutes the job was mine.

• Why do I tell that story? Only to show how this interview was much easier for me with Ron present. He knew it would be easier for me if he were there to break the ice. To this day I can remember how threatened I was, even though there was no real need for those feelings. This is why I understand how you, or any reader might feel, knowing he was going into the immediate presence of the Lord.

I want my presence to make it easier for you. That's my role in this book. I'm going with you. Not that you couldn't do it on your own. You certainly could. However, since this has become a way of life for me, my presence might easily be a comfort to you, especially in the first meeting.

"HERE WE GO!"

I trust you're comfortable. Nice cozy chair. Well relaxed, even though your eyes are open and reading. I wish you could close your eyes for what we're about to do, but you can't. You've got to keep on reading.

1 **Turn on your imagination screen.** Project your image of the "secret place" onto the screen. Go over the "fixins" of the "rendezvous room" until they're vivid in your mind. I'll wait while you do this.

2 **Visualize the Lord.** We're going to do an EXERCISE that can help you visualize the Lord. I want to make sure you have a clear mental picture of Him.

EXERCISE. If you already have a satisfactory picture of the Lord, you need not do this. By that I mean, if you already have a definite PERSONALITY crystallized on the screen, Someone Who is always waiting for you in the "secret place," this won't help you much. But if you've never done any work visualizing the Lord before, you'll appreciate what I'm asking you to do.

All right, let's begin. Look at Jesus on the cover of this book for 5-10 seconds. Close your eyes. Does a similar face appear on your imagination screen? Don't worry if it doesn't happen the first time. Study the cover once more, this time focusing on the face alone for 5

103

seconds. Close your eyes. An image starting to form? You'll get some kind of an outline.

When you study the face a third time, pay particular attention to the hairline . . . the eyebrows . . . the nose . . . the bearded chin. Trace them with your eyes, as though using a pencil. Observe the lines in the forehead. Then close your eyes once more. By now you should be getting a picture of Jesus. It doesn't have to be too detailed. No matter how many people study this picture, no two will project the same image onto the imagination screen.

> **IMAGE.** It isn't necessary to **duplicate** the book cover in your mind. I'm not after duplication. I'm simply coaching you in the **imaging process.** The Holy Spirit will be working with you to see that the picture you project is best for you. It is your willingness to do this that brings the Spirit's help. Since we're working BY FAITH, it is up to us to **initiate the action.** God waits on us to "seek" and "knock" and "ask" (Matt. 7:7). If we sit back and wait for God to take the initiative, He'll let us wait until death overtakes our bodies. He likes for us to exercise our faith. He likes for us to show initiative. Working with a mental image of Jesus is an action step that excites the Holy Spirit.

What, exactly, are we doing? We're crystallizing the Lord's presence in a form **you can project** into the "secret place." Even if you can't put a face to the form, this exercise will FIRM UP His presence. His nearness will be more definite. It pays to exercise in any endeavor. Doing this a dozen times or more will pay off nicely. The Lord's presence will become more substantial, more real, each time you do it.

As soon as you have a firm image, we'll go into the "secret place" together. Jesus will be waiting for us. But just before we do, I'm going to ask Him to help you visualize the scene . . . even as you're reading these words:

"Lord Jesus, my friend and I are about to enter the 'secret place' to enjoy Your presence together. As we enter this precious experience, Lord, would You make it vivid and lifelike by the anointing of Your Spirit. Allow both of us to feel the warmth of Your love as our welcome. Thank You, Lord."

As you read these words, the Spirit will grant you a unique witness. The scene is going to be alarmingly real. Expect it. What's more, something special is going to stir inside you as you sit there reading — the Lord's own excitement. He knows what's coming. He can hardly wait.

FICTITIOUS? Satan may whisper, "Hey, all this stuff is make-believe, it's all phony." But you know better. How come? While Jesus abides in **your spirit**, He is REALLY THERE. Nothing fictitious about that (Col. 1:27). He bids you "come boldly" into His presence (Heb. 4:16). So that can't be argued. And how does a person behold Him? By FAITH. There's nothing fictitious about that either (Heb. 11:1). Neither is there anything phony about the Lord's excitement. You'll feel it.

Walk into the "rendezvous room." The two of us have now entered the "secret place" together. The Lord has been waiting for us. We're standing before Him — by faith. I'll speak first:

"Here we are, Lord. This is my friend (your name)_____. We've come to enjoy Your presence and we want You to enjoy us. Thank You for the warmth of Your Spirit that makes us feel so welcome."

Imagine! The two of us in the Holy of Holies! Such a thing is not possible except with a SPIRIT-ANOINTED IMAGINATION. Consider, the two of us together be-

105

fore the Lord in the "secret place" of the Almighty! Wow! Has this ever happened in your life before? Not likely.

ENTERING THE "RENDEZVOUS ROOM"

the "secret place"/imagination screen

JESUS' PRESENCE BY FAITH

You may wish to drop the book into your lap for a bit while you close your eyes and visualize what is taking place. This is a remarkable moment. The Holy Spirit will help you picture the two of us going into the Lord's presence. The Spirit, Himself, is intensely interested in this action. Even though you're reading a book, you may find your heart beginning to pound.

REMEMBER: WHATEVER SCENE FORMS IN YOUR MIND NOW WILL BE CREATED BY THE HOLY SPIRIT. IT WILL BE THE ONE HE PLANS FOR YOU TO USE DURING OUR TIME WITH HIM. THE PICTURE YOU NOW HAVE OF THE LORD WILL DO NICELY.

Pause for a moment. Just because you're in the Lord's presence, don't feel rushed to speak to Him. This is not like an ordinary situation — this is spirit to spirit. So take a moment to check your spirit. What do you feel? Does not the Holy Spirit indicate the Lord's pleasure? Do you not sense how thrilled He is to have you VISUALIZE Him by faith? Faith of this sort makes Him tingle with excitement. He loves what you're doing. What you're experiencing this very moment is the Lord's delight warming your soul. So bask in it . . . take your time . . . let it fill your being.

TALKING TO JESUS — DIRECTLY

Now it's time for you to speak to Him. By faith He stands before us in whatever form the Spirit has impressed on your imagination. Don't be afraid. There's not one thing to fear. The Lord is thrilled that you have brought Him from the other side of the screen. He feels blessed by it. You can be sure He is excited over meeting you this way. He can't wait for you to speak. Use words like these to get started:

"Lord Jesus, I wasn't sure how I was going to feel, meeting You like this. I thought it was going to be scary, but honestly, it's glorious! I know we're meeting SPIRIT TO SPIRIT, yet here I am giving You a form I can see. This is a big change for me, since I'm so used to thinking of You as being out of sight. Why, I could reach out and touch You!

"Wow, Lord Jesus, this is even better than brother Lovett said it would be. And You know what thrills me most? That You know me better than I know myself, and STILL WANT ME TO COME AND BE WITH YOU. That's precious. Thank You, Lord, for making me feel so welcome, so at home in Your

presence. I can't help but praise You for being such a fantastic Friend and Father to me. You're wonderful! I love You!"

You'll probably get started and then ignore the words I've written here. The Holy Spirit will make you feel so much at ease, you'll be chatting with the Lord from your heart. No kidding, you can't possibly guess the joy this brings to Jesus. It delights Him to have our faith reach "behind the mirror" and bring Him around to our side where we can enjoy Him face to face. Talking to Him like this, man to man, sends shivers of ecstasy through His being.

> **SHIVERS.** You know what it takes to please God — FAITH (Heb. 11:6). Consider the faith it takes to visualize Him in the "secret place." How that must thrill Him. Remember: we're giving FORM to a living person, not to a concept. And we're doing this so we can have fellowship with Him on a face to face basis. The more real He is to us, the more we're going to respond to His presence. I'm sure you can see that. Now if you walked right up to Him (by faith) and said, "Here I am Father, enjoy me!" He'd be ecstatic. He'd love it! You might think yourself a bit brassy, but it would delight His soul. Having loved you to the death, it thrills Him to have you with Him. This is why we must not withhold ourselves from Him or be selfish with our presence.

There's no way I can sit here and predict the words that will flow from your lips as you sense the Lord's boundless affection for you, and behold Him looking at you so longingly. Precious things will pour from your heart to His. But there is one thing you can do that would make His Spirit soar — **a commitment to devote more of yourself to Him.**

THE FIRST LEVEL — COMMITTING YOURSELF

Here's the kind of a commitment you should make — **purpose to spend a little time with the Lord each day to share YOUR PRESENCE with Him**. I put it on that basis, because He never withholds His presence from us. We're the selfish ones. He's the generous one. So it's important that we set aside a few moments each day just to BE WITH HIM.

This time of which I speak is SEPARATE from your regular devotion and prayer time. It is NOT to be used for prayer requests, though the Lord enjoys answering our prayers. **It is to be used exclusively for enjoying Him and letting Him enjoy you.** Its purpose is MUTUAL DELIGHT in each other. Yes, you'll be expressing your delight in the Lord, but you'll do it by praising Him for being such a wonderful Father and Friend.

Some readers tend to skip the preface of a book. If you didn't read the preface of this book, would you turn to it now and read about the little girl who climbed up in her daddy's lap and gave him a big kiss and told him she loved him. That has to melt the heart of any father — even God. No matter how much we think we're grown up in Christ, we're still just wee children in God's eyes. To have us come as little children and say "I love you, Daddy," is perhaps the biggest blessing He enjoys as a PARENT.

With that in mind, listen again to dear brother Paul:

 "... **those who are led by the Spirit of God are sons of God ... and by Him we cry, 'Abba, Father!' The Spirit Himself testifies with our spirit that we are God's children**" (Rom. 8:14-16 NIV).

So as I stand here with you in His presence, **how about making such a commitment right now?** I'm serious. This is the first step a person must take if he's going to DELIGHT HIMSELF IN THE LORD! There is no short cut. And what better time than when we're here together. I'll be your witness. But make it a genuine commitment, one without reservation. It could go like this . . .

> "Father dear, I do love You. I here and now commit myself to greet You each morning when I awaken and to spend _____ minutes with You every day. You really are the greatest 'Dad' anyone could have and I don't want to be selfish with You any longer. I am making this commitment Father, as a first step in learning how to delight Your heart and also to delight myself in You!"

You can read those words right off the page if you like. But be sincere in saying them to the Lord. Determine to follow through with your commitment. Most readers will probably read what I've said, close their eyes, and put the commitment in their own words. The number of minutes you set aside each day should be an amount you can easily manage. If you commit too much time, more than you can spare, you won't keep your commitment. Even if you can only afford 3 minutes a day, do so on that basis. **Once you start, purpose to keep it up for life**. It means so much to the Lord.

ISN'T THAT PRECIOUS?

I trust you made the commitment. If so, you're on your way to great delight in the Lord. How do you feel now? Terrific, I'm sure. The Lord's pleasure over your commitment is intense, and He's letting you know it. You're feeling it. Whenever we do something that truly delights Him, His joy floods our souls.

Say good-bye to the Lord . . .

110

"Well, Dad, this has been great. Though talking with You directly is a little new for me, I really like it. I know it'll get even better as I get used to Your presence and become more relaxed around You. But I'll be back soon, and we can really get to know each other. See you later, Lord."

You and I turn and walk away from the Lord, departing from the "rendezvous room" together. Now that you have Him there, He'll be waiting for you when you're ready to return, perhaps after you finish this chapter.

● What do you think of your imagination now? Fabulous, isn't it! Do you see the genius of our Heavenly Father in giving us such a gift? Just think, in this day when we walk by faith, we can enjoy the REALITY OF THE LORD by means of this amazing ability! See now why I said the highest purpose of the imagination is to visualize the Lord!

The next thing is to **make your commitment a part of your daily routine.**

SPENDING TIME WITH GOD

Did you know this is what Jesus loved to do more than anything else? It's true. He'd get up "a great while before day" and find a solitary place where He could enjoy His Father in the "secret place" (Mark 1:35). Jesus did exactly what I'm teaching you to do. In fact, it was He Who portrayed God as a loving Father to us, and taught us to speak to Him directly . . . "Our Father Who art in heaven . . ." (Matt. 6:9). His love for the Father and the Father's love for us was the basis of His teaching. Believe me, that was brand new in those days.

BRAND NEW. Before Jesus came and changed the

way men were to worship God, believers had only the Jewish program with its outward ceremonies and rituals. While the High Priest went into God's presence once a year, individuals rarely had contact with God at all. They participated in the sacrifices and read from the Psalms. Jesus' death abolished that old method of external worship, replacing it with worship in "spirit and in truth." With Pentecost, believers' bodies became "temples of the Holy Spirit," wherein Christians could retire to the "secret place" and worship God in spirit. They put into practice what Jesus taught them, enjoying INTIMATE CONVERSATION with God for the first time. While this privilege is badly neglected today, you are in the process of making it a part of your life.

INTIMACY WITH GOD— OUR PRIVILEGE ONLY!

JEWISH PROGRAM	JESUS' INCARNATION	PENTECOST JESUS' RETURN IN THE SPIRIT
High Priest intercessor for man in Temple "Holy of Holies"	announced replacement of external worship with internal worship in "spirit and truth"	Jesus our High Priest inside us. Bodies "Temple of Holy Spirit"
NO DIRECT ACCESS TO GOD	death split veil in "Holy of Holies" signifying TERMINATION OF EXTERNAL WORSHIP	DIRECT ACCESS TO GOD FOR ALL BORN-AGAIN BELIEVERS
EXTERNAL WORSHIP		INTERNAL WORSHIP IN "SPIRIT AND TRUTH"

INTIMATE TALK

May I assume you're not used to intimate conversations with God? For some of you that won't be the case. But for many it will be a brand new experience. For the sake of the many for whom this is new, I'm going to include some sample conversations (prayers) based on what Jesus said about our love relationship with the Father. These are merely to help you get started. After you get used to the idea, you'll be carrying on your own "Papa prayers" (intimate conversations) per your closeness to the Lord. So for starters, try these:

"Father, picturing us together, chatting like old friends is new to me. But I realize this is what You want. Thank You for alerting me to this glorious use of my imagination and for the way Your Spirit helps me realize You're actually here with me. What an adventure, Lord! And to think — my visualization of You is going to get clearer and clearer as we spend more time together. This is going to be great, Lord!"

"Lord, here I am again, keeping my commitment, coming to be with You. I'm trying to speed up my visualization of Your presence, so that our times together will be more exciting and enjoyable. Your Spirit tells me You're delighted to have me come and feel at home in Your presence. Thank You, dear Friend, for giving me Your own righteousness so that I don't have to feel like a dirty sinner around You. I'm beginning to appreciate what it really means to be a child of God — and it's nice, Lord, to BE MYSELF in Your presence."

"Precious Lord, as I relax in Your presence, I find my love for You becoming more and more intense. Just being with You and sensing the glory of Your person captures my heart. I gladly reaffirm my commitment to spend more time with You. I want to. I know it's going to help me be the kind of a person You want me to be.

Knowing You love me and are proud of me makes me more determined than ever to live a life pleasing to You. You, Yourself, are having a tremendous influence on me."

"Father, thank You for sealing me to Your heart. Now that I've been with You a few times, I sense Your commitment to me. You really are in love with me, and I feel it. Now I know nothing will ever separate us. What a great Friend You are, Lord Jesus. And I want You to know You are becoming the most important fact in my life. The closer we become to each other, the more I realize I wouldn't want to live without You. You are my life, my joy, my source — even my future."

Observe the increase in fervor? This is what happens when you start getting closer to the Lord. He is such a fantastic Person, His sweetness captures your heart. You fall in love with Him. I mean with a bond you wouldn't believe. **The more you know Him, the more you love Him. The more you love Him, the more He becomes your daily delight.** See — I was serious when I spoke of Christ becoming our obsession.

DAILY DELIGHT

When you first begin to meet with the Lord in the "secret place," you're more apt to be concerned with the process than with Him. This is natural. But as you keep your commitment, you'll find the Lord becoming increasingly real with every visit. **What you're doing at this level is DEVELOPING AN AWARNESS OF HIS PRESENCE, coming to the place where you enjoy being with Him.**

While I have provided some sample conversations, don't feel you have to keep up a stream of chatter. You don't have to say a word to enjoy the Lord. You can sit there and look at Him if you wish. But you do have to

BE WITH HIM. It's important to get used to being in the "SAME ROOM" with Him, and being relaxed. **In time, He'll become as real to you as your husband or wife. When that happens, He'll be your daily delight.** So, discipline yourself to keep that commitment. An exciting awareness of His presence will be your reward.

DO YOU LIKE MUSIC?

He does. If, while you're in His presence, you wanted to sing or hum a song of praise, He'd like that. Contemporary Christian artists have given us some highly devotional songs, and then there are the old favorites. Songs of praise can add a sweet touch to your time with the Lord. Anything you might sing, bespeaking your love for Him would be a blessing. Some of the contemporary ones go like this:

Jessy Dixon's *"Father Me"* — *"I know You're always here, I feel Your hand brush away my tears, and You take me in Your arms and Father me."*

Kelly Willard's *"Jesus"* — *"Jesus, come and take my hand. There is no where else for me to run but straight into Your arms. Wrap my heart with Your love and keep me warm."*

Benny Hester's *"Nobody Knows Me Like You"* — *"More than a friend, someone I could talk to. You put Your arms around me, You bring me through. Though some know me well, still nobody knows me like You."*

Andraé Crouch's *"My Tribute"* — *"How can I say thanks for all the things You've done for me. The voices of a million angels could not express my gratitude. All that I am and ever hope to be, I owe it all to Thee."*

Some of the older songs also bespeak familiarity with the Lord. Consider lines from these favorites:

"What A Friend We Have In Jesus" — *"Do thy friends despise, forsake thee? Take it to the Lord in prayer; in His arms He'll take and shield thee, thou wilt find a solace there."*

"Precious Lord, Take My Hand" — *"When my life is almost gone, hear my cry, hear my call. Hold my hand lest I fall; take my hand precious Lord, lead me home."*

"Leaning On The Everlasting Arms" — *"What a fellowship, what a joy divine, leaning on the Everlasting Arms! What a blessedness, what a peace is mine, leaning on the Everlasting Arms!"*

You don't have to be able to sing; the Lord listens to the **intention** of your heart. Whatever the words, let them speak of your love, your adoration, your worship for Him. Not only will He be thrilled with this outpouring of affection, but you'll find yourself delighting even more in His presence.

KEEPING YOUR COMMITMENT

As you keep your commitment, He will reveal more of Himself to you each day. In time He'll become your dearest Friend. But you must stay with it. You must be faithful. You must be consistent.

At first you may find it difficult to be consistent. Satan will suggest many things that will SEEM more important. **So you'll have to set aside time every day and stick to it.** It will become easier as you "get into the habit."

The chart below is a sample of the one you'll find in the appendix.

DAILY DELIGHT CHART

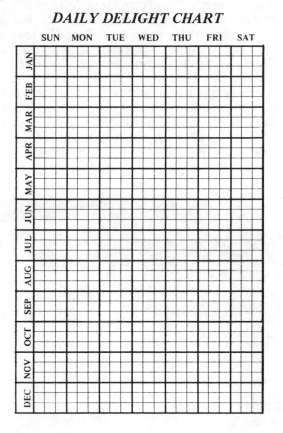

Remove the one from the back of the book and post it in your prayer area. As you meet your commitment each day, check the chart. This way your progress is revealed at a glance. Though I've made the chart for a year, you probably won't need it that long. In time you'll look forward to your meetings with Jesus. It's the DELIBERATE START we need, and the chart is a tool the Holy Spirit can use to prod us until it becomes a habit. At some point, Jesus will be so real, your obsession will keep you coming to Him.

FOR PARENTS. It's amazing how children pick up on spiritual matters. They seem to be so sensitive. Ages 5 and upwards apparently have no problem picturing their Heavenly Father as being inside them, right there waiting to share His love and protect them. Adults seemingly lose this capacity for "fantasy dreams, innocent play and fairy story imaginations," but children LIVE them. How much better to fill children's imaginations with the exciting truths of their Heavenly Father, than with fairy tales. What a head start it gives them on their personal walk with the Lord. So after you have mastered this simple step for yourself, why not share it with your children?

Children can learn early in life to trust in the loving hands of their Heavenly Father.

When Jesus was on earth, it delighted Him to have little children come to Him and climb on Him:

> "People were also bringing babies to Jesus to have Him touch them. When the disciples saw this, they rebuked them. But Jesus called the children to Him and said, 'Let the little children come to me, and do not hinder them, for the kingdom of God belongs to such as these. I tell you the truth, anyone who will not receive the kingdom of God like a little child will never enter it.' " (Luke 18:15-17 NIV)

I'd like to share a letter from a young woman who lost her parents at an early age:

> *"All these years I have often wanted to say to them, 'I love you.' Now that I'm able to give my love, I've wanted to return it to my parents. But they're gone. I couldn't begin to count the times Jesus has taught me that He's my mother, father, sisters and brothers when I need them. He's filled that void in my life.*
>
> *"I visit with Jesus a lot in the 'secret place.' I'd have 'flipped out' a long time ago if I didn't have my best Friend, Jesus. When you wrote about 'Abba, Father,' my spirit cried, 'amen!' I find myself saying, 'I love You, Papa. Papa, I love You!' Just telling Him that makes Him closer to me, and I experience Him more personally, more deeply. I'm so glad the Lord is leading you to show people how to draw closer to Him. He's the best friend we have."*

(Mrs. J. A. — NE)

Isn't it precious to hear a young lady speak of the Lord so affectionately? Clearly the Spirit made Jesus real to her. If you don't feel that way about Him right now, you will before you finish this book. Once able to BE YOURSELF with Him, you'll find yourself weeping and laughing with Him, pouring out your true feelings, for He'll become your closest friend.

Doesn't that make you eager to move on. I know it does.

SUMMARY

Here's what we're seeking to do at this level.

1. We're becoming AWARE of the Lord in the "secret place."

2. We're getting used to VISUALIZING Him.

3. We're committing ourselves to SPEND TIME with Him.

But don't be in a hurry. I know you're anxious to move on to the next level, but you must discipline yourself to stay at this level until you FEEL AT HOME with Jesus. You've got to get used to being in the "SAME ROOM" with Him, and that takes time. So keep your commitment. Give Him that time. Get to the place where you can prop your feet on the coffee table and chat with Him. Learn to be at EASE with Him, fully RELAXED.

Then — when you really FEEL AT HOME with Him, you'll be ready to move to the next level of delighting in the Lord. If you think this level is great, you'll find the next one even MORE REWARDING. But don't cheat yourself. Stay at each level until you're ready for the next one.

Chapter Seven

ℒevel Two-
The Tender
Touch

*At this level we are going to make contact with
the Lord. Not only will we be visualizing Him and
enjoying His presence as we did at the first
level, but **we're going to TOUCH HIM — experience His
embrace — by faith.***

*I mention this to prepare you.
I don't want you offended at the thought of drawing
nigh to God. If you feel uncomfortable or offended
at any point, stop reading immediately. Check
with the Holy Spirit. Ask Him how He feels about
this. Let His witness be the final authority. You
see, my work stands or falls on His witness, so I am
most happy to have you check with Him about
anything you read here.*

 Some months ago, Jim Bakker invited me to appear as a guest on PTL in Charlotte, North Carolina. Sometimes the TV guests are also asked to speak in the 2500-seat chapel at Heritage U.S.A. When I received that invitation, I elected to speak on going into the "secret place" and holding Jesus in our arms.

At the end of my message, I asked those in the audience to close their eyes and **"Come with me into the Holy of Holies."** As heads bowed and eyes closed, I lowered my voice, speaking softly into the microphone.

God's Spirit moved across hearts (especially mine) granting awesome reality to the experience. By faith, each person accompanied me into the "secret place" where Jesus was standing . . . waiting. As I coached, each one took Jesus in his arms. Then, using broken phrases, I led them like this:

"I love you, Daddy. You're the greatest Dad, the best Friend anyone could have. You're the center of my existence — my joy, my strength, my life. Nothing means anything to me without You. I want everyone to know how wonderful You are, how delicious You are! I'm so proud of You I could bust!"

Without exception, everyone there trembled in those everlasting arms as Jesus held them close. They not only hugged the Lord, but gave Him a kiss, too. When it was over and the people raised their heads, tears of joy were flowing down many cheeks. There was a lot of nose-blowing.

Afterwards, Henry Harrison, Jim Bakker's number two man, said to me,

"You know, brother Lovett, that was so precious I didn't want to come out. I just wanted to stay there and bask in the presence of the Lord."

WHAT IT DID FOR THE PEOPLE

The Holy Spirit was good to us that night. Everyone was able to enjoy the Lord in a face-to-face interlude.

For most, it was the FIRST TIME they'd ever been in the "secret place." Never before had they experienced the Lord like that. When the service ended, they swarmed about me to tell me what it was like for them. Out of all that was said, this was the concensus:

> *"I'll never again think of the Lord as Someone so holy I can't be myself around Him. What this did for me was make me realize He's hungry for fellowship with me. Now I can enjoy Him as a close personal Friend, rather than a perfect God Who's unhappy with my imperfections and sins."*

As I listened to the different ones affirm this precious truth, it dawned on me **why** the Holy Spirit had me minister as I did. He was seeking to **break down** the FORMALITY BARRIER believers instinctively create between themselves and God because of their feelings of unworthiness. Satan knows how to use those feelings to make us shove God away. How exciting to hear the people say things like:

> *"What a difference this is going to make in my prayer life. I can hardly wait to get off someplace where I can be alone with Jesus and hold Him in my arms some more! The faith life will never be the same for me after tonight."*

And again:

> *"I doubt if the Lord will ever be the same to me after this. I had always pictured Him as Someone far above me. I never dreamed this kind of intimacy was possible, or that He desired it. Now that I know better, I'm going to enjoy Him a lot more. In fact, I'm sure it's going to be better for both of us!"*

Do you see what they're really saying, what these people actually learned — THAT FORMALITY IS THE

ENEMY OF INTIMACY! They had tasted intimacy with Jesus and loved it. At the same time, they knew the Lord was enjoying them with equal thrill. This is why I said earlier, "Formality separates people, whereas intimacy draws them close together."

Really, what could be more obvious? Try getting formal with your husband or wife and see what it does to your relationship. It definitely won't bring you closer to each other. Similarly, when people are FORMAL WITH GOD, addressing Him as a distant Deity, there's no way they can feel close to Him. Rather, He seems a million miles away.

Well, that night at Heritage U.S.A., the barrier came down. As a result, the Lord now has a nice group of people enjoying Him in a different kind of fellowship. . . a new kind of intimacy. Jesus is the winner.

A NEW KIND OF INTIMACY

In our last chapter you committed yourself to take time each day for becoming MORE AWARE of the Lord. I'm going to assume you're keeping this commitment, working on visualizing His presence and becoming comfortable around Him. As you discover all the wonderful things you've heard and read about Him are true, **you love Him dearly**. The "secret place" is becoming your favorite resort.

● Now we're going to leave the "FATHER/CHILD" stage of your new intimacy with the Lord and move to the next level . . .

THE SECOND LEVEL – TOUCHING
THE LORD BY FAITH

Please remember what I said earlier about our romance with Christ. The love is *AGAPE* LOVE, divine love — love in its purest, highest form. Rid your mind of any carnal notions. Our intimacy with Jesus is wholly spiritual. Jesus lives INSIDE US, and that's the **most intimate union of all.** We're simply learning to DRAW CLOSE to the Lord and ENJOY a precious intimacy that ALREADY EXISTS. But first let's consider. . .

THE ROMANTIC LANGUAGE OF GOD

Do you watch TBN from time to time? Then you have seen "Mom and Dad Billheimer" bringing Bible studies to the viewing audience. I'm a Paul Billheimer fan. He has given me permission to quote from his unpublished work, **THE UNIVERSE IS ROMANTIC.** But first let me say, he believes the sole purpose of the earth is to produce and nurture an eternal companion, "the bride of Christ," for God's Son . . . that the love Jesus has for this church is all consuming. He further believes the relationship between Jesus and His church IS RECIPROCAL, that is, a two-way street.

To quote him:

> *"The principal ingredients of romance are love and adventure. If anyone has any doubt that the relationship between Christ and the church is romantic, all he needs is to read and understand the Song of Songs (Song of Solomon).*
>
> *"When the intimacies described in this passage are understood as pointing ultimately to the relationship between Christ and His church-bride . . . it elevates those intimacies into the hallowed and sublime, while in no sense depriving them of the present romantic connotation.*
>
> *"Notice the language of romantic love. 'Let Him kiss me with the kisses of his mouth: for thy love is better than wine' (S.S. 1:2 KJV). 'Behold, thou art fair, my love . . . (vs. 15). 'He brought me to the*

banqueting house, and his banner over me was love' (S.S. 2:4). Now notice this passage, 'Thou art beautiful, O my love . . . turn away thine eyes from me . . .' (6:4,5). This is the language of infinitely blissful affection. It reveals the Bridegroom so entranced by the beauty of His bride that He is lost in unspeakable transport. The Bridegroom is carried away by such overpowering rapture and delight that He is overcome, even to the point of a trance."

It may be hard for you to accept, but this is the way Jesus feels about you. He is in love, and it is romantic love elevated to pure and exquisite delight. Believe it or not, you're involved in a "love affair" that is basically the proper explanation for this world. In everything God does, He has in mind the glorious day when Jesus will receive His "bride," and the "love union" will be consummated. That's the big purpose behind the human program. Jesus loves you with a passion that consumes Him.

So when I speak of meeting Him in the "secret place," you can be sure your presence . . . your words... your touch . . . bring infinite satisfaction and pleasure to God.

NOW LET'S GO TO HIM

This time we're going into the "secret place" to **shower our affection on the Lord, and by faith, we're going to touch Him.**

 Relax. Turn on the screen of your mind, and project the "secret place" and the "fixin's" of the "rendezvous room" onto the screen.

 Visualize the Lord. Crystallize your mental image of Him just as you have practiced. He's waiting for us.

3 Now the two of us are entering the room.

For the moment, don't do anything. Just watch. I'm going to leave your side and approach the Lord. Observe what I do. Witness the joy in His face. See me reach out and take His hand. No, not to shake it, though that would be fine with Him. I hold it for a moment and then put it next to my cheek. You can tell it thrills Him. Then I move His hand from my face and kiss it. He deserves this adoration.

The Lord doesn't just stand there. He responds. As I continue to hold His hand, He reaches out to me with His other hand. He strokes my head a few times — then draws me to Himself. As I lean against His shoulder, a shiver goes through me as I recall how the apostle John leaned against the Lord in the same way at the Last Supper (John 13:23-26).

Then — my soul is satisfied as those everlasting arms encircle me and I cuddle next to the One I adore. His love caresses my spirit, and I respond:

"Lord Jesus, I love You. I worship You. Thank You for Your precious blood that makes it possible for a sinner like me to feel at home in Your embrace. Your loving arms about me make me realize nothing matters but our relationship. I am absolutely nothing without You. You are my joy, my life, my future . . . everything."

NOW IT'S YOUR TURN

Move from your position and come stand beside me before the Lord. Don't be afraid. Don't worry about your sinfulness either. His blood has already taken care of that. You needn't feel unworthy in any way, for He has made you as righteous as Himself (2 Cor. 5:21). Besides, you're one of His sons. So c'mon, relax, be yourself and feel at home.

That's great.

Now it's **your turn** to touch Him.

Reach out and take His hand. Go on, don't hold back. He WANTS you to do this. In fact He needs it. Take a good hold. That's fine. Cling to it for a moment, there's no hurry. Believe me, the Lord Jesus is enjoying every bit of this. He's feasting on it.

Now press the back of His hand to your lips. Kiss it tenderly. Good. Now press it against your cheek. If your tears run down on His hand, don't wipe them off. They're liquid affection — to Him.

You're doing this by faith, BUT HE'S NOT. He's not working at the faith level. He's ACTUALLY soaking up your affection. **What you're doing via your imagination, HE'S LITERALLY ENJOYING IN THE SPIRIT!** So cast away your reluctance! Release yourself! Lavish yourself on Him! He deserves all the affection you can shower on Him, and responds to it. IT'S REAL TO HIM.

Be ready for this. His other hand reaches out to you. Feel the tenderness as He strokes your head. Let His powerful arms draw you next to Him. How's that for a loving **crush**! Great, isn't it! Can you feel His passion for you as He holds you close to His mighty chest? Guess the first words the Holy Spirit will put on your lips . . .

"Lord Jesus, I love You."

As you are tenderly gathered in those loving arms with your cheek pressed against His, you'll want to say more to Him. No matter what words come from your lips, you can be sure they'll be loaded with affection. You may find yourself speaking like this . . .

"It's fantastic to be in Your arms, Lord Jesus.

128

My deepest longing has been to get as close to You as I could. I love our spirit-to-spirit relationship. Being in Your arms like this fills my soul with joy."

Once you begin talking to the Lord you may not find it easy to stop. The Holy Spirit may prompt you to do and say things that could startle you:

 "Lord, if You don't mind, I'd like to hold You in my arms. I know You created me for Your pleasure, and I'd like to give You a big hug, and kiss You on the cheek."

"IF YOU DON'T MIND!" To Him that's funny. That's what He died for. You'll meet no resistance from the Lord. You'll feel His arms instantly relax, so that you might embrace Him. Your own spirit will tell you He's thrilled with every bit of this. You'll feel His delight as you clasp Him to yourself.

You'll be amazed at the EASE with which you find yourself kissing Him on the cheek. The truth is — **you won't be able to help yourself.** The blessedness of the moment will simply bring it out of you. You'll want Him to have this outward token of your affection, and when you do, there'll be an earthquake in your soul. Your whole being will tremble — in the spirit.

KISS. To some, the idea of kissing the Lord on the cheek will seem strange. But He's used to it. In the days of His flesh that was the custom. You may recall how He rebuked Simon the Pharisee, saying, "**You gave me no kiss . . .** "(Luke 7:45NAS). Kissing is a powerful expression of affection and admiration. This is why parents kiss their children; why lovers and sweethearts make such a thing of it. It's full of meaning. Besides, it does something for you to kiss Jesus this way — **it'll make your relationship with Him sweeter and more intimate.**

129

Kiss Him once and your fellowship will never be the same. No longer will He be a distant God to you, but a kissable friend.

How many Christians, do you think, lavish affection on Jesus like this? Not many, you can be sure. To them, God is TOO ADULT to enjoy human displays of fondness and affection. Hugging Him is a childish act to them. Yet, while they deny HIM this pleasure, they easily slobber all over a wife or sweetheart or child, and think it's great. But when it comes to Jesus, they won't show Him the tiniest bit of affection. What a shame. Not only is it a thrilling experience to the Lord, but it brightens up the believer's fellowship with Him. What's more, He absolutely loves it.

● Did you ever think you'd be holding the Lord in your arms, telling Him how much you love Him? You can do it any time you please — BY FAITH.

ALONE WITH HIM

I'm going to step out of the "secret place" and leave you alone with the Lord. There are intimate things you may want to say to Him now that you have Him in your embrace. This might be a good time to **put the book down and spend the next few moments hugging Him, showering affection on Him, and basking in His presence.**

● Good. Now say good-bye to your "Lover" and leave the "secret place." You can return later.

YOU ARE BETROTHED

Remember when you were engaged? You couldn't wait to be with your fiancé. Every minute away from him/her was anguish. Days dragged while you waited for the big day when you could be married and spend the

130

rest of your lives together. That's how I want you to feel about Jesus. You ARE BETROTHED to Him (2 Cor. 11:2). It is a spiritual "engagement."

How cruel if you refused to return His love. But I know you **will** return it. You want to enjoy Him as your "Lover" and Friend, delighting in your total access and intimacy; while He, at the same time, is eager to return your love in the spirit. This privilege of meeting Him in the "secret place" is TEMPORARY. Holding Him in our arms and showering our affection on Him by faith will soon be a thing of the past. We must enjoy it while we can.

When will it end? On our "wedding day" in the sky. Then you see, it will all be BY SIGHT, not by faith. Never again will we be able to love Him by faith. Everything will be different then. Once the earthly program is over, a **different kind** of fellowship with the Lord begins. It will no longer be PRIVATE, as it is now. When the marriage is "consummated" in the spirit, our sweetheart time will be just a happy memory.*

SO LET'S ENJOY THE COURTSHIP

To receive the greatest delight from your times with Jesus, think of Him as your Fiancé. Take Him in your arms. Let Him hold you in His arms (of course by faith). Pour out your affection on Him. Kiss Him and thrill to the warmth of His embrace. Tell Him you love Him, can't stand to be without Him . . . can hardly wait for the "wedding day." You see, He's eager, too. From His position He can see the "eternal honeymoon" — the face-to-face joy of eternity.

---

* It is beyond the scope of this book to discuss the "wedding in the sky" and the "eternal honeymoon." But you'll find both ideas explained in the author's book, **LATEST WORD ON THE LAST DAYS** (chapters 9 and 12).

Each of us will have his own way of loving the Lord. He made us all unique, so that He could revel in the way each of us UNIQUELY cares for Him as a "Lover." An INFINITE LOVER needs to be loved in infinite ways.

● Brother Lawrence would be proud of us. You can see what we're doing — PRACTICING THE PRESENCE OF CHRIST. We're doing exactly what the famous monk of Lorraine did, though carrying it to a higher level.

Anything a person would do well requires practice. You can practice the Lord's presence to the place where He becomes **more real** than the things around you, **more real** than your family and friends, yes — even **more real** than your problems. When that happens, He becomes YOUR OBSESSION. To know Jesus that intimately is to get HOOKED on Him — even as He is on you. Wow, does the romance get exciting then!

SWEETER AS THE DAYS GO BY

Now that you've learned to delight in the Lord, I want to make sure you **include Him in your daily routine.** It's one thing to take a quiet moment where you can relax, shut out the world and fellowship with Him in the "secret place." That's what you did on level one. However, it's something else to be able to go about your daily business AND STILL enjoy the Lord as intimately. This is what you'll be doing on level two. This is what He **really wants:**

"As you therefore have received Christ Jesus the Lord, SO WALK IN HIM" (Col. 2:6 NAS).

Let's put another verse with that idea:

"And whatsoever ye do, do it heartily as to the Lord, and not unto men" (Col. 3:23 KJV).

How does a believer do things **"as to the Lord?"** There's only one way — DOING THEM WITH HIM. The truth is, the Lord aches to be **included in everything we do. He longs to be a part of the tiniest details of our lives.** One of the ways we hurt Him most is by leaving Him out of our activities. We must not let this happen.

Here's where we are so far:

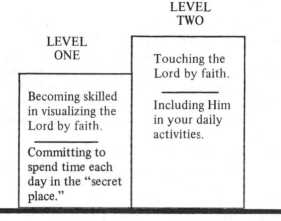

LEVEL
TWO

LEVEL
ONE

Touching the Lord by faith.

Becoming skilled in visualizing the Lord by faith.

Including Him in your daily activities.

Committing to spend time each day in the "secret place."

Below are some ideas for including the Lord in the day's activities. As you read, I'm sure He will bring to mind other circumstances in which you can include Him. The more, the better.

FIRST THING

One of the best ways to SWEETEN your life in Christ is to greet the Lord FIRST THING when you arise in the morning. Sure, you may sit on the edge of the bed, yawn a couple of times and rub your face before you speak. But even if you say, **"Hi Lord, I'm awake . . . I think,"** He'll delight in that kind of closeness. Then, after you've washed your face, grabbed a cup of coffee/breakfast drink and are waiting for the cobwebs to lift, say to Him, "I'm thinking You have something special for us today, so I'll try to be ready and watching for it."

MARRIED?

If it is your custom for you and your mate to have Bible study together in the morning, as Margie and I do, do it WITH HIM — include Him. How? By making comments when you come across something that extolls His mercy, kindness or generosity. Compliment Him when He does something super in the Bible. If you said, "Wow, You're sure gracious, Lord." He'd appreciate that you noticed, and bothered to tell Him. Should you read a portion that exalts His wisdom and power, praise Him from an astonished heart. "Lord, are You ever smart!" Such praise from His own is exhilarating.

I call this "OPEN-EYED INTIMACY!" You haven't shut your eyes to pray. You're speaking to Him as though He were right there in the room with you and your mate. You can see how being included in your fellowship would make Him feel.

After you've finished reading the Word and spent time in prayer, give Him another moment. "Anything on Your mind You'd like me to ask about?" Then wait. Don't be surprised if the Holy Spirit puts someone or something on your heart He wants mentioned in prayer.

● You're a housewife? Housewives can enjoy a special treat by taking Jesus shopping. He likes going down the aisles of a market with you. It's fun for Him to help you select items. As you look at different products, speak to Him under your breath, "See anything that looks good, Lord?" Or, "What do You think my husband would like tonight?" Then be ready for inspiration. You see, Jesus has good ideas for meal planning. To consult Him on such trivial matters creates a familiarity that delights

134

Him. He loves it. It makes Him what He wants to be — your intimate Companion.

"Lord, help me pick out a surprise meal for my husband."

● **You're a husband?** Heard the slogan, "Things go better with Coke?" Well, Christians have turned that to say, "Things go better with Christ!" One of the best places to prove that is on the job. The Lord likes nothing better than to walk out the front door with you, get in the car and fellowship on the way to work. If you sing on the way, He'll join you. Best of all, if you hit a snag at work all you have to do is say, **"Okay, Lord, how are we going to handle this?"** Then expect His help. You won't be disappointed.

SINGLE?

Some prefer to remain single in this day and age. They feel they can better answer God's call on their lives by remaining unmarried. My older daughter prefers the single life. Here's her testimony:

"My romance with Jesus does more than take the place of a husband. With Jesus as my 'Lover' I don't miss a husband. I have been told I'd make a good nun, but one doesn't have to be a nun to enjoy the benefits of being 'espoused to Christ.' God has called me to paint for Him, and I'm determined not to let anything interfere with that call.

"By remaining unencumbered with a husband and children, I am able to concentrate on Jesus and the task He's given me. You might say my romance and intimacy with Him are expressed in my paintings. I talk to Him constantly as I paint. I ask Him, 'What should I paint next? What colors should I use? How do You want this to look?' And He directs me. It's as though the Lord's hand were on mine, guiding it as the brush touches the canvas.

*"Not only does He help me with my painting, but takes leadership in every (I hope) aspect of decision-making — finances, food, clothing, housing, car, medical expenses, and most of all, **spiritual** problems. I can look back on my life and honestly say He has **never** once let me down. I let Him down, but He never lets me down.*

"There are times when I get lonely, but on those occasions I slip into the 'secret place' and tell Jesus about it. I tell Him things I want no one else to know. There isn't anything I can't discuss with Him. Soon I feel better. Time with Jesus causes loneliness to leave.

"I encourage all single Christians (and married ones, too) to express themselves in some form of creativity as a love-offering to the Lord."

Linda Lovett

LEFT ALONE?

Death and divorce create a time of need. To know the joys of good parents or a precious mate and have them taken away, produces a painful void. Without leadership or security, many become disoriented.

Who will fill that void? You know — JESUS!

When Margie's dad died, a void was left in her mother Edith's life. Edith sought to fill it by working with us in the ministry. Yet, no matter how busy she became, you could tell she missed her mate. However, since I was her pastor, she looked to me for spiritual guidance. I was able to teach her how to enter into the "secret place" and enjoy the Lord as a personal, intimate Friend. He soon became her obsession, the center of her life.

Everyone watched the change that took place in her face when the Lord replaced her loss **with Himself**. She became a **woman aglow**, spreading cheer wherever she went. That same privilege awaits all Christians who have been left alone.

THE CENTER OF EVERYTHING

When we get to heaven, what do you think will be the center of life there? Jesus, of course. So why not get used to that fact NOW? Wouldn't it be great to get to know the Lord **so well** in this life, that when you meet Him in the air you could smile and say, **"Hi Lord, this is great, just what I thought it would be!"** I mean, be casual when you say this, finding it but the continuation of a fabulous friendship that had already begun on earth. Wouldn't that be terrific!

A FORETASTE OF HEAVEN

It's so sweet to be close to Jesus. You know, if people don't want to HUG AND KISS Him now, why would they want to in heaven? Surely location can't make any difference. It would seem that if Jesus is not that sweet and precious to us now, why would being in heaven make any difference? We should ACHE to be as close as possible to the One Who is more than life to us.

I'm persuaded that when you discover how much HE NEEDS THIS, you will agree with me. You may further agree that **what we do with Him in this life, determines to a great extent, our ability to enjoy Him in the next.** You see, God is not only screening out those who will TRUST Him and OBEY Him, but also those who will DELIGHT in Him (Psa. 37:4).

That's what awaits us in LEVEL THREE. It may startle you, even shock you to think the Lord NEEDS our affection, comfort and praise. But once over the shock, I'm sure you'll be glad to give it to Him. In fact, when you learn what it does FOR HIM, you may give your life to it.

We'll see.

Level Three-
Ministering To The Lord

*In levels one and two, we learned how to draw nigh
to the Lord — how to "cuddle with Christ." This was
primarily for OUR OWN SAKES, that we
might enjoy Him and the blessedness of
those "everlasting arms."*

*While that brings us unsurpassed delight, it
must not be the only reason for meeting the Lord in the
"secret place." In level three, you'll find that the Lord
has needs, genuine needs only we can meet. You'll
see how we can be a great blessing to Him
for the express purpose of meeting those needs.*

LEVEL
THREE

LEVEL
TWO

Ministering to
the Lord,

LEVEL
ONE

Touching the
Lord by faith.

Ministering to
5 areas of the
Lord's needs.

Becoming skilled
in visualizing the
Lord by faith.

Including Him
in your daily
activities.

Committing to
spend time each
day in the "secret
place."

Chapter Eight

Our Lord Needs Us

". . . He has chosen us in Him before the world was founded, to be holy and blameless in His presence. In love He predestined us in Jesus Christ to be His sons . . . for the praise of His glorious grace with which He has freely favored us in union with the Beloved." (Eph. 1:4-6 MLB)

As a boy, I lived in a small town in the middle of the San Joaquin Valley in central California. A super rich man, who practically owned the city, lived in a big white house on a knoll just outside of town. Everybody catered to him. His wealth and power commanded everyone's respect. As kids will do, we'd speculate as to how great it'd be if we had all that money. Why, we could buy anything we wanted. We thought Mr. Z_____ was the luckiest man in the world.

140

That's the way I thought of him until an incident changed my mind.

One day, after I'd been out hunting in the ravines and vineyards, I decided to cut through Mr. Z_____'s peach orchard to get home earlier. My path took me directly behind the mansion. I didn't expect to meet a soul, but whom should I run across, but Mr. Z_____ himself, sitting on a box behind a shed at the rear of the big house. I wasn't ready for what I saw.

The man was crying.

When he looked up and saw me, he turned his head to hide his tears. At first, I thought he was going to scold me for trespassing. He was a crotchety old geezer. But when I saw him so broken, it was clear I had nothing to fear. In fact, my feelings shifted. My heart went out to him. I wanted to help him if I could.

He must have sensed my sympathy, for he decided to talk. Maybe a boy was the right person. Anyhow, he needed to talk to someone and I was the only one around. As he began, his pent-up feelings gushed out and I got the sad story.

THE RICH MAN'S PROBLEM

Mr. Z_____ confided that his heart was broken out of loneliness. He was suffering "the rich man's syndrome." He had oodles of relatives and all kinds of people who claimed to like him, yet all any of them wanted was to get their hands on his money. Everyone, it seemed, was **after something**. Tearfully he confessed **he couldn't name a single person he felt truly loved him for himself.**

As he sat there, broken hearted, sympathy oozed out of me. Growing up without father or mother, I knew about loneliness. From then on, I never thought of Mr. Z_____ as the luckiest man in the world.

See where I'm heading? Of course.

In many ways "the rich man on the hill" is our picture of God. This is the way most view Him.

Aren't we inclined to think of Him as super rich and powerful, living in the big white house atop the hill? Don't we see Him surrounded by immense wealth, attended by myriads of angels eager to do His bidding? You know we do. We're always referring to His "cattle on a thousand hills" (Psa. 50:10). Don't we look on God as a "warehouse operator" who somehow has to give us everything we ask, because we request it in Jesus' name? You know we do.

"So how in the world," we ask, "could He possibly NEED anything? What in the world could 'lil ole me' give to the One Who has everything? Nothing!" is **our** answer. Consequently we never think of God as needing anything from us at all.

BUT OUR LORD DOES HAVE NEEDS!

I hope you won't be offended, but I DON'T believe God has everything He needs – **or He wouldn't have made us!** I'm convinced He has great needs, genuine needs, vital needs **only we can meet.** In spite of His wealth and power, it is true for Him, as it was for Mr. Z_____, there are things money cannot buy. When it comes to friendship and love, these can never be secured by force, no matter how much power a person has. **They have to be given.** And this applies to God as well as anyone else. He has no other way to get them, and **we're the only ones who can give them to Him.**

> **SHOCKED?** You could be startled at the thought of God having needs, but I hope you'll hear me out and not be hasty in your judgment. I assure you having needs will **NOT DETRACT** from His greatness in any way. The problem is this: few believers scarcely spend any time with the Lord these days. They're so caught up in a "hit and run" existence they don't get close enough to Him to learn whether He has needs or not. They have no chance to learn of His cares, thoughts or desires. However, once they come to know Him as a FRIEND, and stop thinking of Him as a WAREHOUSE MANAGER, they begin to understand Him and know how to treat Him. They discover He really does have needs. But until that time, He remains more like an EMPLOYER, whose workers care more about the paycheck, than the man who's paying them. If you'll reserve judgment and stay with me, I'm sure you'll be glad you did.

As I speak of the Lord as having needs, bear in mind I'm referring TO A PERSON. He's an individual, having intellect, emotion and will; Who, regardless of His wealth and power, has the **same basic needs** as do we, who are created in His image.

● I'm going to list what I consider urgent needs of the Lord. I know you'll be listening for the Spirit's voice. If

143

what I am saying is true, His witness will be loud and clear.

① BEING LOVED FOR WHO HE IS

God's NUMBER ONE need is to be loved for WHO HE IS, *not* for what He has or for what He can do for people. He needs to be loved as an individual. If that isn't given to Him, the hunger remains. The truth is He's starved for it, even desperate. Calvary tells us **how** desperate (as we saw in Chapter Two). So, being loved is first on the list.

What could be worse than being a lover with no one to love? And no one to love you in return? That's the way it was before God made man — and it had to be torture. There was NO ONE on whom He could pour out His love and have it returned. This is why He made us His image, like Himself, so we could receive His love and return it. **Of all creatures, only you and I can love God as He yearns to be loved.**

If you're still not convinced, consider what Jesus said to one of the scribes when asked, "What commandment is the foremost of all?" Jesus answered:

 "The foremost is, 'Hear, O Israel! The Lord our God is one Lord; and you shall love the Lord your God with all your heart, and with all your soul, and with all your mind, and with all your strength' " (Mark 12:28-30 NAS).

Why do you suppose we're told to love God with all of our being? Because it is His **greatest need**. That commandment is not simply a passing thought. It's a DEMAND on us to meet God's craving for love because He's so in love with us.

② HE NEEDS ATTENTION AND PRAISE

We're not used to thinking of God as AN EGO, or HAVING AN EGO. Yet, in truth, He is the biggest Ego of all. "I AM THAT I AM," is the most egocentric statement anyone can make. Yet that's the way God revealed Himself to Moses at the burning bush (Ex. 3:14). Because of this, the Bible commands,

 "Let everything that hath breath praise the Lord. Praise ye the Lord" (Psa. 150:6 KJV).

You're familiar with man's ego. From whence does it come? From being the image of God. We're made like our Heavenly Father. We need attention and praise, because that's the way we're designed, like Him. **He needs honor and tribute,** so do we. There's nothing wrong with having an ego or satisfying it — legitimately.

Some would say it is sinful to seek ego satisfaction. But that is wrong. The ego has to be satisfied or an individual is left empty and frustrated. It is **HOW** the ego is satisfied that is important. It can be done in an EVIL way or in a GODLY way. If it is done through lying, boasting or exploiting others, then of course it is wrong. But if a person's ego is satisfied by legitimate praise, praise that is EARNED, then it is a blessed thing. Having an ego is necessary. How it is satisfied is what makes the difference. **Certainly God has RIGHTFULLY EARNED every bit of praise we could give Him.**

Consider those tremendous scenes in Revelation where the reader beholds the throne of God and those waiting upon Him. Like this one:

 "The four and twenty elders fall down before Him that sat on the throne, and worship Him that liveth for ever and ever, and cast

their crowns before the throne, saying, 'Thou art worthy, O Lord, to receive glory and honor and power: for Thou hast created all things, and for Thy pleasure they are and were created' " (Rev. 4:10,11 KJV).

Those before the throne KNOW how worthy He is. Everything in them compels them to praise and adore God — not because He commands it — but because He merits it, deserves it.

❸ HE NEEDS TO BE COMFORTED

Comforted? Yes, God definitely needs to be comforted. You see, when you love as He does, it's easy to get hurt. Any woman who has given herself to a man knows how true this is. When she commits all the way, her heart is right out there where it can be stepped on, leaving her wide open for abuse. Many a woman knows the pain of having someone tread on her heart.

So it is with God. His heart is on the line.

Remember Diogenes? He went about Athens with a lamp in his hand, looking for an honest man. Well, our Lord Jesus goes about with His heart in His hand, looking for people who'll love Him. He travels the streets, cities and homes, pleading with people to call Him "FRIEND" and enter into a love relationship with Him. **And He is ready to deliver the blessings of heaven on those who will fellowship with Him.** Driven by a super human thirst and hunger for companions, He puts His heart on the line. "Love Me," He begs, "My heart is right out there. Don't step on it! Love Me!"

But alas, as you know, **His heart gets stepped on plenty.** When you consider the bulk of those for whom He died will have nothing to do with Him, that has to **hurt.** He suffers plenty. Rejection is one of the most painful

146

things a person can endure, and the Lord is rejected by multitudes daily.

It was Jesus Who said . . .

 ". . . broad is the way, that leadeth to destruction, and MANY there be which go in thereat: because . . . narrow is the way, which leadeth unto life, and FEW there be that find it" (Matt. 7:13,14 KJV).

Observe the "MANY" and the "FEW." Of all the billions to inhabit the earth, only a FEW have any interest in the Lord, though He would that none should perish (2 Pet. 3:9). The many, it seems, clearly will have nothing to do with Him. That's got to be painful.

But that's only part of the Lord's hurt.

Not only do rejectors pierce Him with sorrows, but you and I hurt Him too. I won't spend time on our backbiting, our stinginess with Him and divisiveness over doctrines. But it all adds up to a lot of grief for our precious Lord. This is why Paul felt it necessary to say, "GRIEVE NOT the Holy Spirit of God, whereby ye are sealed unto the day of redemption" (Eph. 4:30 KJV). The hard truth is, He not only has to suffer rejection by the masses, but we — HIS VERY OWN — also give Him much grief.

GRIEF. Do you find it strange to hear the apostle Paul speak of our "grieving" God? We're used to thinking the cross put an end to all of Jesus' suffering; that once it was over, His pain had come to an end. But it isn't so. The Lord is STILL SUFFERING. Sensitive to Jesus' continued suffering, the apostle referred to his own agonies as filling up that which is lacking in regard to Christ's afflictions (Col. 1:24). In other words, he sees Jesus as still suffering for His church. But what about the church could bring Him such grief? Ah, the sight of His children gossiping and dividing over petty matters, when He longs for them to BE ONE in spirit (John 17:20-23). What pain the fragmentary church of today must bring our Lord!

You've been hurt. None of us goes through life without some pain. Surely you know what it is to be comforted. To have a friend put his/her arm around you, tell you he knows how you feel and is standing with you helps a lot. With the Lord receiving abuse from all sides, comfort has to be one of His greatest needs. Isn't it fantastic to think we're **able** to comfort Him? Honestly, don't you feel a yearning to put your arm around Him and comfort Him? I know you do.

❹ HE NEEDS AFFECTION

The Lord is an affectionate person. That's why we're affectionate. Affection is spirit. It doesn't come in buckets or by the pound. It doesn't belong to the flesh, though it can be displayed through the flesh. On the last level, level 2, we learned to be affectionate with the Lord. **He needs to be hugged and kissed the same as we. He longs for AFFECTIONATE INTIMACY with each of His children — by faith.**

Think how you'd feel if no one ever put his arms around you and told you he loved you — in all your life. Yet many of God's children have never once given this affection to Jesus. His passion for every believer is the same, and His yearning for affection from each one is the same. God is love, and it is vital to realize affectionate people crave affection — and thrive on it. Jesus longs to be cuddled.

❺ HE NEEDS TO FEEL WANTED, NEEDED AND INCLUDED IN WHAT WE DO.

148

Because He's God, we tend to leave Him out, thinking it's all too petty for Him. Because of that . . .

"IT'S LONELY AT THE TOP."

You hear that phrase often these days, especially in political circles. Certainly there are times when it must get awfully lonely for God. Barring Him from our routine activities, we keep Him stashed in the "God room." There must be moments when He feels like an aged widower committed to a rest home, waiting for His kids to get around to visiting Him. Children can be cruel, you know — especially when it comes to taking parents for granted.

Someone standing off, watching the way we treat the Lord, might easily conclude He was a real bother. Someone we'd just as soon have out of the way — **until we needed Him**. Then, of course, they'd see us get very serious about Him — **as long as the need lasted**. Once it passed, we'd forget Him just as quickly.

So our God sits there, lonely most of the time. Hardly anyone thinks of HIS NEEDS — needs to feel NEEDED . . . WANTED . . . INCLUDED. What could be worse than feeling like an OUTSIDER where your own children are concerned?

For some reason we don't seem to understand the hunger that fills His being, His deep longing for fellowship with us. If we did, we'd spend long periods in prayer. We'd make every effort to lift Him out of His "loneliness" and include Him in the routine of our lives. To our shame, we don't bother. The truth is we're **too busy** — most of the time.

Sure, we ask His blessing at mealtime. We bow our heads to say grace, but once that's out of the way, we pick up our knives and forks and all thought of the Lord

149

vanishes from our minds. He may get those first few seconds, but that's it. He's excluded from our fellowship around the table.

You and I, in downright indifference, ignore the Lord for hours at a time while we do our own thing. We raise families, pursue careers and plan for old age — as though He didn't exist. To us THESE are the important things, while fellowship with the Lord is reserved for Sunday and Wednesday night. Am I exaggerating? Do not these receive the PRIORITY in our lives? You know they do.

He's left out.

We have lots of good times from which we exclude the Lord. It doesn't matter to us that **He ACHES to be included in the tiniest details of our routines.** Nothing we do is trivia to God. He is vitally interested in everything we do, not wanting to be left out of a single thing.

 "Are not sparrows two for a penny? Yet without your Father's leave not one of them can fall to the ground. As for you, even the hairs of your head have all been counted. So have no fear; you are worth more than any number of sparrows" (Matt. 10:29-31 NEB).

The God Who sees every sparrow fall and counts the hairs on our heads, is eager to be involved in the most minute details of our daily lives.

● I haven't attempted to PROVE God's needs. If I'm on target, the Spirit Himself will satisfy your heart about it with a powerful witness. It is my task to STATE them — His to prove them. So let me ask: "Doesn't the thought of meeting His needs feel good down deep inside? Doesn't the mere mention of God's needs make you want to shower your affection and attentiveness on Him?" I know it does.

I don't have to sell you on this. From within your own spirit will come the LONGING to comfort Him, and let Him know what He means to you. Once you begin, the PURE DELIGHT filling your soul will be all the proof you need. So please don't reject the idea of God's needs until you've lavished your affection on Him at least once. The echo of His pleasure in your spirit will do the convincing, not I.

OFFENDED?

Does it offend you to have me say God needs our attention and affection? Inclined to argue the point? Of course, if you insist it is impossible for God to need anything or anyone, **you'll never do anything to comfort Him, or minister to Him.** Instead, you'll continue to think of Him as a WAREHOUSEMAN Who simply doles out blessings impersonally, because it's His nature to do so. But you see, God is not just a giver and a blesser. He's an individual who likes to be treated AS A PERSON.

I'm convinced Christians need to be aroused to the fact that OUR GOD DOES HAVE NEEDS, and **we're the only ones who can minister to them.** Who, may I ask, will comfort the Lord if we don't? Angels? Well, maybe they'd have to, if no one else cared enough.

WOULDN'T BE THE FIRST TIME

Remember when Jesus knew the cross was but hours away? And how He led His disciples to the garden of Gethsemane, saying, "My soul is exceeding sorrowful, even unto death?" (Matt. 26:38). Then, with Peter, James and John, He moved to an inner recess of the garden where He asked them to keep watch while He prayed. Going a "stone's throw" beyond them, He dropped to His knees and began to plead with His Father.

151

"O My Father," He cried, "if it be possible, let this cup pass from Me . . ." (Matt. 26:39). We'll probably never know the agony He suffered there, but we do know His anguish was so great His sweat was like "great drops of blood" falling to the ground (Luke 22:44). And how did the disciples carry out their watch? THEY FELL ASLEEP.

Then what happened? While they dozed, AN ANGEL appeared from heaven and assumed the task of ministering to the Lord (Luke 22:43). When it was over, the Lord rose from the ground to find His disciples sleeping. Disappointed, He scolded them. "What, could ye not watch with Me one hour?" (Matt. 26:40). Those three boys missed their big chance to minister to Jesus when He needed them. So the task fell to an angel instead.

THE DISCIPLES REALLY MISSED THE BOAT

Can you imagine what it would have meant to Jesus to have been comforted by His own? What if they had surrounded Him as He cried out, gently putting their hands on His shoulders and saying . . .

"We don't really understand what You're suffering, but we sense it's for us, and we love You for it. If there's anything we can do to help, we're ready to do it. But we want You to know we truly care for You."

Wow! Those words would have sounded sweeter than a chorus of angels. Obviously there was nothing they could do, other than be there. But then, that's all the angel could do. The point is — the angel was there! That's what counted. It would have meant everything to Jesus had those disciples considered how much their love and concern would have helped. Yes, they missed the boat — and we do too, if we feel there is no place for ministering to the Lord.

CAN WE REALLY HELP?

Wondering if coming to the Lord simply to share your presence with Him really helps Him? Really comforts Him? Let me relate something that happened to President Lincoln.

 One afternoon an elderly lady kept her appointment to see Mr. Lincoln. As she entered his office, the president arose, helped her to a seat, then asked,

"How may I be of service to you, Madam?"

"Mr. President," she replied, "I know you're a busy man. I haven't come to ask anything of you; just to bring you this box of cookies, of which I understand you're very fond."

The president said nothing for a moment, during which tears came to his eyes. Finally he raised his head and spoke to the woman:

"Dear lady, I thank you for this thoughtful gift. Believe me, I'm greatly moved by it. Since I've been president, thousands of people have come through those doors demanding things of me. But you're the first who's entered this office asking no favor, but bringing me a gift. I thank you from the bottom of my heart."

In the same way, we are a powerful blessing to the Lord when we come into His presence simply to shower our affection on Him and tell Him we love Him. It's a thrill for Him to find us concerned for HIS NEEDS, rather than our own. That's what real friends do. What joy it must bring when we come to GIVE HIM OURSELVES, expecting nothing in return. That has to bring tears to His eyes.

So again, here are His needs:

1. He needs to be loved for Who He is.

2. He needs attention and praise.

3. He needs to be comforted at times.

4. He needs affection.

5. He needs to feel wanted, needed and included in what we do; not left out.

Learning HOW to minister to His needs is next!

Chapter Nine

How To Minister To The Lord

"And the child Samuel ministered unto the Lord . . ."
(1 Sam. 3:1 KJV)

Before I was saved, God blessed me financially. I didn't have to work if I didn't want to. So, when I was saved and began to enjoy a sweet relationship with Jesus, I wanted to know more about the new life I had entered. Margie and I would fire up the coffee pot, spread out our Bibles and spend hours in the Word.

Sometimes we'd break out laughing at our discoveries. Other times we'd cry. Many times we'd be in awe at the exciting things the Spirit would reveal. We felt we were walking through a diamond field, privileged to pick up gems wherever we found them. Sometimes I'd nudge Margie, "I wonder what the neighbors think when they hear us!" It was hard to contain our joy when we ran across a "biggie." We had FUN with our Father, sometimes "cracking up" with laughter.

FUN. Perhaps I should explain my use of the word "fun." Some believers don't see how it's possible to have fun with the Lord. They don't even like the word used in connection with the Christian life. So I hasten to observe that you and I are FUN —LOVING creatures. He made us that way, and we're His image. We shout our heads off at ball games and jump up and down over competitive sports. Why, many of us think a church picnic or potluck dinner is fun. Everybody has fun whether hunting, fishing, sailing, hiking or sunning at the beach. We all like good times, finding joyful delight in a range of activities. That's what I mean by fun. I DON'T mean in the sense of boozing, dancing or off-color entertainment. For me, discovering things in God's Word is as exciting as flying; and to me, flying is fun!

Spending delightful hours in the Word with Margie brought me steadily closer to Jesus. Every time we'd come upon a nugget, we'd pause to discuss it with Him, thanking Him for His wisdom and for sharing His great plan with us. Time after time, I was sure I heard Him chuckling over my bug-eyed amazement at His genius. You can see how intimacy with the Lord came early in my Christian life. He was drawing me into it.

LIKE ON THIS OCCASION

One day, as I was studying the book of Samuel, I came to the place where it says, "AND THE CHILD SAMUEL MINISTERED UNTO THE LORD" (1 Sam. 3:1 KJV). It was the word SAMUEL that first drew my attention. That's my middle name. People call me SAM. (You can too, if you like.) But as I lingered at the verse the other words, "MINISTERED UNTO THE LORD," suddenly leaped from the page.

Now that was a new idea.

I had always viewed the Lord as ministering **to me.** But this was the other way around. Then I was struck

157

by another thought, "Is it possible the Lord has needs the same as we? Does He need ministering to the same as we?" Of course — that was it! Since He has the same feelings we do, He must have the same needs. I had never thought of Him as needing us as much as we need Him.

I felt like a modern day Samuel when Margie and I began including the Lord in our fun. It began, of course, with good times in the Word. We sensed we were ministering to His longing when we included Him in our discussions and laughed with Him when things were amusing. We were having fun — and so was He!

After the Spirit alerted me to the idea that God might have needs, I began to discover them here and there as I read through the Word. My feelings became quite different when I read, for example, a passage like Jesus weeping over Jerusalem,

". . . how often I have longed to gather your children together, as a hen gathers her chicks under her wings . . ." (Matt. 23:37 NIV).

In those words I saw His yearning to draw His own close to Him.

When Jesus would embark on a special mission, He didn't go alone. He always had close friends with Him. In the last chapter, we saw how true this was on that fateful night in the garden of Gethsemane when He asked the disciples to keep watch with Him. Then there was the "transfiguration of Jesus." Remember? He took the same three (Peter, James and John), wanting them to be with Him while He conferred with Moses and Elijah atop the mount (Matt. 17:1-9). He seemed to NEED their company.

Once I tumbled to the truth of God's needs, the Holy Spirit was relentless in leading me to minister to the

Lord. It didn't come overnight, naturally. He gradually schooled me for the task, drawing me continually to the "secret place." Finally I was holding the Lord in my arms, showering my affection on Him.

IT IS BECAUSE OF WHAT IT DID FOR ME AND FOR HIM THAT I SHARE IT WITH YOU. I WILL MOVE GENTLY, GIVING YOU TIME TO CHECK FOR THE SPIRIT'S WITNESS. IN NO WAY DO I WISH TO IM- POSE MY IDEAS ON YOU.

BACK TO THE "SECRET PLACE"

Here we are again. Once more I'll ask you to take a deep breath . . . relax . . . and make yourself comfort- able. Get set for a return visit to the Holy of Holies ("secret place"). This time you'll be going in alone. You don't need me anymore. This is strictly between you and Jesus. Before you go in, let me ask God to anoint your imagination:

"Precious Spirit of God, please prepare ____ (your name) 's heart for this meeting. Will you quicken his/her imagination and fill his/ her mind with the reality of our Lord Jesus. I ask You to move across his/her heart, overrul- ing anything that would keep the imagination from doing its highest work. Amen."

SPIRIT. Not used to addressing the Holy Spirit di- rectly? Does it bother you or seem out of order? Well, just because I have that liberty doesn't mean you have to do the same. It's my conviction that the SAME PERSONALITY exists in the Trinity (Father, Son and Holy Spirit). For myself, I can address one as easily as the other. Usually when I want something **done**, I address the Father. When I yearn for **intimacy**, I address the Son. When I seek the **anointing**, I speak to the Spirit Himself. But if

159

this conflicts with your practice in some way, by all means pray in the manner most comfortable for you. In actual fact, I'm sure we all enjoy the SAME WITNESS no matter which member of the Trinity we address.

● All right, by faith I'm expecting the Spirit to anoint your imagination. You're now set to go into the Lord's presence. It won't be new ground. You'll be in a familiar place. The mystery will be gone.

 Turn on your imagination screen and project the "secret place" onto the screen.

 Visualize the Lord. Bring your mental image of Him into focus.

 Enter the "rendezvous room."

 Make yourself aware of His presence.

There's the Lord, waiting. See the smile on His face? He knows why you have come. Enjoy that smile, it's your welcome. You're more comfortable this time, for now you and the Lord are good friends. Speak freely as you greet Him:

"I'm back, Lord Jesus. I love being in Your presence, and that's because I adore You. I think You're fantastic! It thrills me to be in Your arms and have You minister to me. You make me feel wanted and complete. When You hug me and tell me You love me, I eat it up. You really satisfy my soul.

"But this time, Lord, I'm here to minister to You. I'm starting to realize You have needs too. This is new for me, having blessing flow from me to You. But I'm not just going to learn theories about ministering to You. I'M

160

GOING TO DO IT! I'm here to put in practice what the Spirit is teaching me. If You
didn't need me, You wouldn't have created
me. So I'm going to minister to You Jesus,
and bring You all the joy and satisfaction I
can."

ACTION

All right my friend, move across the "rendezvous
room" toward the Lord. That's it. As before, take Him
in your arms. Yes, He'll embrace you at the same time.
Don't be shy or feel you must say something to Him as
you do this. Just let Him squeeze you to Himself for a
moment. Bask in the pleasure of His presence. Enjoy
Him.

Okay, by now you should be relaxed in His arms.
He'll help you relax by pressing His cheek against yours
and stroking your head. What a super experience! Isn't
it great to be in His arms, enjoying that loving crush!
Now you're ready to . . .

MINISTER TO HIS NEEDS

Let's begin with the one I listed as His FIRST
NEED . . .

❶ LONGING TO BE LOVED FOR WHO HE IS.

Give the Lord a big hug. Speak to Him something like
this:

"Lord Jesus, I delight in the glory of Your
personality. You are holy and true, faithful
and just, merciful and kind, gentle and generous. You are so patient and long-suffering,
completely impartial, you have no favorites,
You are changeless, eternal. I find You to

be ALL these things, for You've showered these graces on me again and again. I know what You're really like — by experience. I could say plenty about Your overwhelming kindness.

"This time, Lord, I'd like to dwell on Your faithfulness. You have faithfully provided for my needs. You've been faithful to help me when I'm tempted. When I get low, You're there to pick me up. When I'm left alone, You're there to enjoy. And may I say, You are fantastic company. You said You'd never leave me nor forsake me — wow! Do You ever keep Your Word (Heb. 13:5)! But there's one particular area in which Your faithfulness is incredible; the way You are faithful to forgive me when I confess my sins (1 John 1:9). God, how I love that! Honestly, Lord, You're absolutely amazing!"

See what you're doing? You're appreciating Him for WHO HE IS. You selected **one item** out of that whole list of glories. You could easily spend hours on His faithfulness alone, citing one specific after another. But you'd be there all day if you did.

Believe me, it thrills the Lord to have you recognize the glories of His personality, and name them one by one. What's nice, you have actually experienced them. This is not "soft soap." You love Him deeply after discovering He really is all those things. This is downright ADORATION. You appreciate Him as a super individual. He's someone you can't get enough of. This adoration is the by-product of being overwhelmed with His greatness.

Be ready for His response.

When you're in the "secret place" holding the Lord in your arms and enjoying Him, **the voice of the Spirit can**

be quite distinct. At first you may not hear it. That's because you're used to listening with your ears, rather than your heart. But you'll pick up on it. In a short time, you'll be able to receive communications from God's heart to your heart. It won't be long before you will be having delightful chats with Him.

> **VOICE OF THE SPIRIT.** We're speaking of spirit-to-Spirit communication. There is no actual sound, of course. Your spirit picks up what His Spirit is saying. We saw in an earlier chapter that your spirit is unconscious (subconscious). Therefore the conversation is NOT DIRECT as in ordinary conversation. The communication comes by way of IMPRESSIONS or CONVICTIONS that arise from within your own spirit. It's the language of the heart. I realize this is difficult to grasp, but after you get used to it, you and the Lord will be chatting back and forth. It will be as though the two of you were sitting together in a swing on the front porch. At times there may be no conversation at all. That's okay. Close friends enjoy each other without a word passing between them. This is the kind of EASE God would have us enjoy around Him.

LISTENING WITH YOUR HEART

We're going to do an experiment. I've asked the Holy Spirit to coach me as I write down what His response will be to your words of ministry. He is the One Who is going to benefit the most from this book. He knew you'd be reading it at this moment. True, what I'm saying here is only a sample of His response. Nonetheless it is what He led me to put down.

My next words are for your **heart**. You're going to practice hearing with your spirit. As you read these words, consider them as God's response addressed to your spirit:

"Thank you, my precious child, for coming. You don't know how blessed it is to hold you in My arms. I love hugging you. To have you close to Me, wanting to minister to Me is a great comfort. I'm thrilled that you love Me AS I AM. It was kind of you to mention the things you like about My personality. You're right, I can't change Myself. I am the way I am and people have to accept Me that way. Therefore it pleases Me greatly to have you love Me FOR WHO I AM — and even want to be like Me. I know why you've come, and I love you for it."

Stop reading. Close your eyes. Check your spirit. I mean take time, listen. Can you detect the "wee small voice?" Really listen. If you don't sense His witness, read the response again, remembering you're still in His arms. I'm convinced He means for you to hear His voice in your heart.

❷ HE NEEDS ATTENTION AND PRAISE

We spoke of the Lord as having an ego, as being an ego. We know this because that's what we are. If our egos need to be fed, so does His. We like to be congratulated when we've done a good job. We like to have our achievements acknowledged. We like approval from others, especially when we've done something outstanding. We even like to be complimented for the way we look and the clothes we wear. We love to be admired, applauded and esteemed — particularly when we deserve it.

Nobody lives in a vacuum. We all crave attention. Look at the awards people give (Nobel prize, purple heart, Academy awards, athletic awards, etc.). The medal and trophy business is big. From the highest to the lowest, we all seek attention and praise, whether a 1-year-old child learning to walk, or a president trying to balance the budget.

164

But here sits our "poor God," the greatest achiever of all. Yet few bother to credit Him or praise Him for the magnificent things He has done. His achievements top all others. His past performance is spectacular — creating the world and everything in it, including us, His image. On top of that, He provided at a great sacrifice, a way for our total redemption. Where's His medal for that?

And He's still at it: maintaining the earth's laws, cleansing us from daily sin and ministering to our needs. What's more, He has future plans where we again behold His unselfishness. He intends to share His kingdom with us, making us kings and priests (Rev. 1:6). He wants us to reign with Him forever, and who knows what He has in mind after that! If we need a hero to worship, a friend to adore, we've got the BEST in Jesus.

No matter what a Christian might say in praise of the Lord, it could never be flattery. **He's earned it** — the hard way. So as you speak your praise of Him, there's no way you can overdo it. Just open your heart and let it pour out like this:

"Lord, You once said, 'There is none good but God.' As far as I'm concerned, there's none who deserves praise but You. You are the most worthy of all, more worthy than anyone to receive honor, glory, attention and praise. All others fade away by comparison. I could never run out of praise for You Lord, for everything I am or hope to be I owe to You.

"Besides, you fill my life. Thanks to You, I know who I am, why I'm here and where I'm going. Thank You for wanting me, wanting me here with You in the 'secret place' and also in Your kingdom. I don't deserve to be here, let alone share in Your inheritance. But I praise You that You want me. The feeling is mutual, Master. In fact, nothing makes sense for me unless You're the center of it. You are my life, my future, my hope. I could never praise You enough for all You've done for me, though I'M GOING TO TRY in the days ahead."

Once you get started, it's hard to quit. It could take years to list all the things for which God deserves our praise — maybe an eternity. That's probably what we'll be doing (among other things, of course). You're going to find yourself wanting to do it more and more right now. You're getting to know Him so intimately, praise just seems to roll from your lips. You're doing it because you WANT to, not because you HAVE to. Praise is the by-product of your love for Him!

❸ HOW TO COMFORT THE LORD

We've already seen how the Lord gets plenty of hurt. Not only by those who reject Him, but by His own as well. Because He's so big hearted and can take it, doesn't make it any less painful for Him. He'd never complain, but you know the ache has to be awful. What a shame for us to withhold, especially when we know the PAIN OF REJECTION is so fierce. We've all tasted it in one form or another — and it hurts!

Because our Father is LONG-SUFFERING by nature, He's willing to endure this pain until the **last person** in the "Lamb's book of life" has been saved (2 Pet. 3:15; Rev. 21:27). Just because He's willing to bear it, doesn't mean we shouldn't seek to comfort Him.

To me it is marvelous that we can bring comfort to the Lord Jesus — by faith. In the spirit we enter into the "fellowship of His sufferings" and minister to Him

(Phil. 3:10). I hope this doesn't sound irreverent, but there's a sense in which we ought to take good care of our Father. He's the only God we have.

All right, He's still in your arms and your lips are close to His ear. You're going to COMFORT HIM, and you feel great about it, for He has already responded warmly to your expression of love. Say:

> "Father, while I can't feel it, I know it must hurt terribly to have people reject You and despise Your sacrifice. You long to draw everyone to Yourself and lavish good things on them, but most won't have anything to do with You. That's got to be excruciating. Through what little I've suffered, I know rejection is about the worst pain of all.

> "There's not a lot I can do to ease Your pain, dear Lord, except to hold You in my arms. I pray my arms are a comfort to You. I know what it means to have You hold me in Your arms when I'm hurting, so now I am returning the favor. For what it's worth, Lord, I comfort You now and love being with You. If there's anything I can do to ease Your hurt in any way, tell me, and I'll do it."

Now that is a genuine ministry to His hurt. Holding the Lord in your arms lets Him know you are forgetting yourself and thinking of Him. Your presence — and your arms — feel good. Believe me, He draws great comfort from the fact that one of His children is aware of His pain and wants to minister to Him. It helps more than we can comprehend.

GOD'S RESPONSE

There's no way for the Lord to remain impassive to

such tenderness and concern. Your devotion and affection evoke an outpouring from within His being. He's an emotional Lover. As you become more skilled in SEEING BY FAITH, the Holy Spirit will enable you to detect tears of joy streaming down His cheeks. Your spirit will pick up His voice:

"Precious child, when I began this program of creating sons and daughters, I knew there'd be a price I'd have to pay, and that price was pain. But I chose to pay it, because I knew the joy it would bring would be worth any sacrifice. Having you hold Me in your arms and saying those precious words of comfort confirms My decision. I know I did the right thing. My joy is great because of your ministry to Me. You've made it all worthwhile."

To have one of His own say, **"I sense Your hurt, dear Father, and I want to do what I can to ease the pain"** blesses God's soul beyond description. I can't begin to put His joy into words, but you'll feel His "shiver of satisfaction" as you hold Him in your arms.

❹ HE NEEDS AFFECTION

Back in level 2, we learned how important affection is to God. We can't live without it. And since we're made just like Him, we know He can't live without it either. Affection is a vital need in our lives, and in God's too. Angels can't fill that need, as we've seen. Only we, who are created in His image, can satisfy His craving for spiritual intimacy.

So give Jesus a BIG HUG and tell Him:

 "You are the Lover of my soul, the Light of my life. I love You so much, I can hardly wait for the day when faith will be no more and we'll be together in eternity. But for now, it

thrills me to minister to You by faith, for I
love You. I trust my words are like candy and
the squeeze of my arms like a fragrant bou-
quet. You are the most precious Friend and
Lover a person could have. You are my delight, Lord Jesus — all day long. Hold me
Lord, and let me know You delight in me also."

Linger for a few moments in His arms and feel by
your spirit the great satisfaction your ministry of affection brings Him. I assure you His soul drinks it up like a
deer at a fresh flowing spring. When you learn in the
spirit what it means to Him, you'll want to shower your
affection on Him day by day.

5 HOW TO MAKE HIM FEEL WANTED, NEEDED AND INCLUDED IN WHAT YOU DO

When I go flying, I let Jesus know I want Him along.
When I go to buy something, I ask Him to accompany
me. When Margie and I are out shopping or dining together we tell Him it is no fun for us unless He joins us
and takes part in our fellowship. We want Him in on
everything whether joy or disappointment. We do this
because we know He longs to be included.

When we let hours go by without so much as a word
to Him, we're excluding Him from our activities. It's not
fair. True He watches over us, monitoring the tiniest details of our lives, but that's **not the same as being wanted and included.** We should continually invite Him to go
here and there, and do this and that with us. All it takes
is, "C'mon, Lord, let's go."

Are there times when I forget Jesus? Yes, I'm a-
shamed to say. Sometimes I get so busy working FOR
Him, I ignore Him. If an hour or so goes by, I'm usually
embarrassed when I suddenly realize what I've done.

169

Then, of course, I have to say, "Sorry, Lord. That's selfish of me, I know. But I'm working on it." And He's so gracious about it. Never a hint of criticism. What a Friend!

I find the best way to do this is to speak to Him just before I begin any kind of work or errand. For example:

"Lord, Margie's been asking me to fix that leaky faucet for some time. I think I'd better do it today. Want to help? We can chat while we fix it, and You can give me advice if I get stuck. Things always go better when You work with me."

That's just an illustration. There are dozens of things we all do in the course of a day that would thrill the Lord to be included and NEEDED in getting them done. When we let Him know we WANT Him and NEED Him, it ministers to His soul.

If you were a prison warden and wanted to discipline a troublesome inmate, the worst punishment you could give him would be SOLITARY CONFINEMENT. It's bad when you're locked up, not allowed to see or speak to another person. In effect, that's what we do with Jesus when we exclude Him from our daily routines. I won't say any more on that. I'm sure the Holy Spirit will point out instances in your routine where the Lord should be included **by invitation.**

Okay, let's leave the "secret place" for now. I'm sure the Spirit has taken what I've written and is already speaking to you about various ways you might minister to the Lord. The biggest obstacle will not be your understanding, but your flesh. Your spirit is rejoicing in all this, but getting your flesh to cooperate could be something else. But we can overcome the flesh by being systematic in getting started.

A SYSTEMATIC START

On a piece of paper, put down the FIVE AREAS of ministering to the Lord's needs, or tear out the page in the appendix. Post the page in a conspicuous place where the sight of it will be a reminder.

You may not wish to start off with all five at once, so choose **one area of need**. Then deliberately insert the Lord's need area you have chosen into your daily schedule. Do it for a week. The following week, add another. By the fifth week, all 5 areas are incorporated in your walk with the Lord. In the process, the Holy Spirit will show you all sorts of unique ways to delight God's heart. There may be other needs the Lord might lay on your heart to do. By all means add those to your list. You're going to love this — I know it's going to fill your life with a new joy.

PART OF THE INNER CIRCLE

Once a believer samples the thrill of ministering to the Lord and then lives to be a blessing to Him, he joins that "inner circle" (those closest to Jesus). I want you to be part of that select company, along with Peter, James and John. Those who know you will see the change in you. They'll definitely hear a new ring in your testimony, as is true of these two friends, also part of the "inner circle."

From Betty:

"When I was first saved, I knew I needed Jesus. I hungered for Him. But I didn't dream He felt the same about me. The Lord used you to help me fall completely in love with Him. Now Jesus and I have become super friends and we're very intimate. It's so good to kiss His cheek and let Him embrace me. But the best part is going to Him to love Him and comfort Him. In return, He tells me how much He loves me and embraces me over and over. I can't get enough of Him and He can't get enough of me. We talk and talk. We hug and hug. We hold hands. I could go on and on about our laughter and intimacy, but you know exactly what I mean."

From Joan:

"I was fasting and listening to your cassette on ministering to the Lord. On the 4th day, I was in prayer and an amazing thing happened. I found myself in the 'Holy of Holies' and the Lord was so real to me. At first He ministered to me in such a sweet way, my heart wrenched and almost broke for love of Him. Then what I'd heard on the cassette came over me and I realized He needed my ministry to Him. Oh, how I longed to do that. In a flash I pictured myself sitting in His lap, holding Him close to my bosom. What a thrill! Who can describe it! I've had many thrills in my lifetime, but nothing to match this! Praise God, we can draw nigh to Him . . . We can minister to Him!"*

● We've covered precious ground together. You've discovered brother Lawrence's secret — how to minister to the Lord. It transformed his life. It will transform yours. Tasting the thrill of bringing joy to Jesus can easily become an obsession. It's a consuming thing to know Him intimately — and minister to Him.

THE BEST PART

It wouldn't be right to convince any reader that Christianity was somehow LIMITED to fellowship with Jesus in the "secret place." But it is the BEST PART and the starting point for what we want to do and be

---

*Would you enjoy being able to close your eyes and lean back while the two of us go into the "secret place" together? I have prepared an 80-minute cassette entitled **HOW TO MINISTER TO THE LORD.** It enables you to stretch out on a recliner and by means of my voice and your imagination, accompany each other into the Lord's presence. Your imagination works TEN TIMES better when you can **relax and visualize.** This kind of help does wonders for your fellowship with Jesus.

173

in Christ. Let me illustrate with Mary and Martha, the two sisters of Lazarus. This family was greatly loved by the Lord.

One day, when Jesus was in the village of Bethany, Martha made Him welcome in their home.

THE BEST PART (Lk. 10:42)

 "She had a sister, Mary, who seated herself at the Lord's feet and stayed there listening to His words. Now Martha was distracted by her many tasks, so she came to Him and said, 'Lord, do You not care that my sister has left

174

me to get on with the work by myself? Tell her to come and lend a hand.' But the Lord answered, 'Martha, Martha, you are fretting and fussing about so many things; but one thing is necessary. The part that Mary has chosen is best; and it shall not be taken away from her' " (Luke 10:39-42 NEB).

You get the point, don't you? If we never learn to enjoy the Lord, personally, intimately, on a one-on-one basis as we've just seen, we miss the best part. We become MARTHAS, serving the Lord out of duty, rather than delight. The order is important. We must FIRST become MARYS, able to delight in Him as companion and friend. THEN AFTERWARDS, to become MARTHAS, with our obedience the by-product of falling in love with Him.

While the Lord wants and expects obedience, He wants it to flow from hearts set aflame with a passion for His presence. Obedience that begins with holding the Lord in your arms and appreciating His loveliness is the kind He really wants. If you never become intimate with Jesus, serving Him will always be a DUTY, never a DELIGHT. It was delight, you recall, that transformed brother Lawrence. It is DELIGHTING IN THE LORD that will transform you . . .

AND . . .

. . . a day is coming when you're going to need to know how to rush into the "secret place" and thrill to the safety of those "everlasting arms." That day is not far off . . . as we see . . . NEXT.

Chapter Ten

The Bully On The Block

"And he was allowed to make war against the saints and to conquer them, and authority was given him over every tribe and people and language and nation." (Rev. 13:7 MLB)

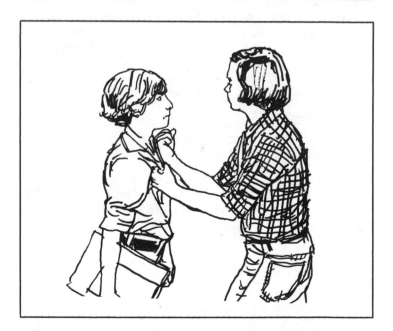

When I was a boy we had a bully on our block. Big for his age, he took great delight in lording it over the rest of us kids. If you got fed up with his pestering and defied him, he'd use it as an excuse to clobber you. On the other hand, it bothered him when you didn't react. Then he'd torment you until you did, and again he'd clobber you. It was a no-win situation when he was in the mood to give you a bad time.

Since I was a skinny little kid, he had no trouble throwing me to the ground and putting his foot on my chest. While he never broke any bones or anything like that, I was often bloodied and my clothes were torn. That was as bad as it got. Still it was painful and humiliating. So, when I'd see him in the distance, I'd always change course to get out of his way; an inconvenience, but better than getting shoved in the dirt.

One day I was sitting on the front porch with grandpa, and here came the bully. I moved close to grandpa as the bully lumbered by on the sidewalk. He looked in my direction, but kept going. He wasn't about to bother me as long as I was with grandpa. I remembered how impressed I was upon realizing grandpa's presence was my security, my safety.

The point?

Any day now, a super bully is going to appear on the block of the world. **That bully will be ANTICHRIST!** The Bible says he will show up in the last days. You've heard that, I know, but you may not know much **about** this man. So let me share a bit concerning him.

> **ANTI.** In the English language when we speak of something as being ANTI, it means "against." But in Greek, the language of the New Testament, it has a different meaning. In Greek it means, "in place of," or "instead of," or "in the room of." So what we're really considering is a SUBSTI-

177

TUTE CHRIST, not someone angrily shaking his fist at the Lord. The man called ANTICHRIST wants the adoration, praise and worship that belong to the REAL CHRIST. Since he is NOT the Christ himself, he will have to TRICK the world into thinking he is. Thus he will be a PRETENDER, relying on **deception** to gain from men that which is due Jesus alone. Were he **hostile** toward God, he'd be recognizable at once. But as a DECEIVER, he will pass himself off as the true Christ. So we're not looking for an enemy of God to appear, rather someone pretending to be God's Son.

Few argue when I say **the REAL antichrist is Satan — the devil himself.** He has always wanted to be God, still does. He wants the honor and worship due the real Christ, even if he has to PRETEND to get it. But the devil NEVER ALLOWS HIMSELF TO BE SEEN AS HE REALLY IS. He always masks himself; always works through others. Therefore we can expect A MAN to appear who will be sold out to Satan and energized by his power. That's who antichrist is — SATAN'S MAN.

But this man will NOT BE OBVIOUS in his approach to the world. He's going to be extremely subtle. So perfect will be his PRETENSE, the whole world will be taken in by him. He's going to fool all of mankind, all that is, except "the very elect" (Matt. 24:24).

SETTING THE STAGE FOR ANTICHRIST

To get the world ready for this man, "the spirit of antichrist" (the spirit of Satan), has been working in the affairs of man to set the stage for this counterfeiter. The apostle John, writing at the end of the 1st Century, spoke of "the spirit of antichrist" as being operative in his day. Just as God is busily working in the hearts of men to get them ready for Jesus, so is Satan busily preparing the way for his man. When the time is ripe (God controls the timing), the devil's man, ANTICHRIST, will pop up on the political scene (2 Thess. 2:3,4).

WHEN THE BULLY APPEARS

 "And it was given unto him to make war with the saints, and to overcome them: and power was given him over all kindreds, and tongues, and nations" (Rev. 13:7 KJV).

Look at this fellow, would you. He's a brute. A few verses further, and we read he's given power to do great wonders, even to the calling down of fire from the sky. With supernatural power of that sort, it's no wonder he can deceive the entire world. But notice his enemies — **the saints! The church!** The bully is out to "do in" every Christian he can find. Please note he has the power TO OVERCOME! This is going to make it rough for every true believer on earth.

When we read further, we learn those whose names are written in the Lamb's Book of Life (that's us) will recognize him for who he is, and REFUSE TO WORSHIP HIM. This will so enrage him, he will issue orders, commanding everyone who refuses to worship his image to be killed (Rev. 13:15). **So we're talking about a bully with supernatural power who's out to get us.** A man doesn't have to be a genius to realize we're headed for tough times.

YET, IT'S GOD'S PLAN

Jesus made it perfectly clear, "In the world ye shall have tribulation" (John 16:33). Tribulation and Christianity are partners. We live in a God-hating world. As long as we're in these bodies, we can expect tribulation. It's part of the package. There's no way to grow up in Christlikeness without it (Rom. 5:3). Thus for the church to have such an enemy as antichrist, and face the kind of tribulation he'll pour out is not unusual or abnormal.

When you consider the powerless condition of the church today, so wedded to the world it no longer has an effective testimony, **you can't help but think it is going to take some serious tribulation to get her ready for Christ's coming.** She's far from ready now. Here in the United States it costs nothing to profess Christ. But this is a church at rest. And a church at rest in this world is abnormal. It's a phenomenon.

What's worse, few believers have any time for the Lord. Almost none take Him seriously. To the average Christian it would appear that everything from baby-sitting to social security is more important than He. Lack of tribulation, in America at least, has generated a host of evils within the church. As one looks back over the history of the church, it's clear she always flourishes under trial. It refines her every time. Even to the most casual observer, her tribulation is long overdue.

TRIBULATION, BUT NOT WRATH

It's one thing for God to refine His people with fiery tribulation; quite another for Him to vent His wrath against her. That He won't do. Why? The Lord Jesus has already born the wrath of God for every believer. He has already suffered God's wrath in the Christian's place. **Therefore it is unthinkable that He would visit His wrath on those purchased by Jesus' blood.**

The apostle John tells us the WRATH OF GOD is going to be poured out in the **final hours** of the tribulation. It will come in the form of the "seven last plagues" (Rev. 15:1). For that reason, nearly all prophetic writers (myself included) distinguish between the **wrath of Satan** and the **wrath of God.** With few exceptions, these writers insist **the church** must **NOT ENDURE THE WRATH OF GOD.**

180

As for the church tasting the fury of the bully (antichrist), many scholars feel it is absolutely necessary for her to endure SOME TRIBULATION if the "bride" is to make herself ready for the "marriage of the Lamb" (Rev. 19:7). The Lord wouldn't want her as she is now. She simply isn't ready for Him. It is my conviction the church is headed for some REFINING FIRE before the Lord summons her to join Him in the sky. And when will that be? In my view (and I can be wrong), it will occur JUST BEFORE God's wrath is poured out on this unbelieving world. If you want to put a label on me, call me a PRE-WRATH RAPTURIST.*

WAR ON THE SAINTS

Terrible things are going to occur at the hand of antichrist. Some of us will be seized, tortured perhaps, in an attempt to get us to deny Jesus and accept the mark of the beast. Antichrist's agents will be everywhere, armed with awesome power to seek out true believers and slay them. Even if we handle it well, it could be rough watching our children abused. We ought to be teaching them how to stand up for Jesus while we can.

Few will escape. Betrayers will be everywhere. Concerning these days I'm describing, Jesus said a man's enemies would be those of his own household:

"Now the brother shall betray the brother to death, and father the son; and children shall rise up against their parents, and shall cause them to be put to death" (Mark 13:12 KJV).

Frightening? And how. No wonder the apostle John says, right smack in the middle of the antichrist passage,

---

*For a full discussion of antichrist's appearance and the author's view of the rapture, refer to his book, **LATEST WORD ON THE LAST DAYS.**

"Here is the patience and the faith of the saints" (Rev. 13:10b)! And when it is all over, John sees a large crowd gathered with Jesus on Mt. Zion and comments;

 "... and I saw the souls of them that were be-headed for the **WITNESS OF JESUS**, and for the **Word of God ...** " (Rev. 20:4 KJV).

See — it appears that's the way most of us are going to exit this life, and be a part of that precious crowd.

HOW WILL YOU HANDLE YOURSELF?

Beheading could be antichrist's favorite method of execution. However I suppose that's immaterial. The point is, **how will you handle yourself?** Here's the scene: your family and friends are gone. You're alone, waiting your turn to be executed. How will you feel then? How will you handle yourself?

See now why I mentioned the bully and the safety of grandpa's lap? There's only one place to be — **safe in the arms of Jesus.** You slip into the "secret place." There He is — arms outstretched to embrace you. **Let the bully do his worst.** The presence of the Lord is so real you're not aware of anything but Him.

Your body will die, of course. But don't let that bother you. A glorious thing occurs the moment death strikes — **it shatters the mirror in your mind.**

SHATTERING THE MIRROR

 "Now we see only puzzling reflections in a mirror, but then we shall see face to face. My knowledge now is partial; then it will be whole, like God's knowledge of me" (1 Cor. 13:12 NEB).

Death is not the terrible thing men make it out to be. It is the FINAL ADVENTURE of the faith life. The devil has sold us a bill of goods, using the "fear of death" to intimidate mankind (Heb. 2:15). Death is an exciting experience. You see, when the body dies, **the mirror/TV screen separating us from Jesus crumbles, dissolves.** And we simply **cross over** to the other side **into His ACTUAL PRESENCE.**

With the screen shattered, it is no longer a matter of faith. What was ON THE SCREEN as a faith experience suddenly becomes AN ACTUAL experience. I mean, you're REALLY in Jesus' arms. You see, **what was faith for you was never faith for Him. He really had you in His arms all the time, only you weren't aware of it.** You took it by faith. But with the mirror gone, **faith has been replaced by fact.**

You've heard of testimonies where dying people have said **"I see Him! He's taking my hand!"** Now you know what is happening. As the fleshly barrier is dissolving (the death process), Jesus is already reaching out His hand to escort the Christian over to His side.

For a brief moment as death was approaching, it **was** a matter of faith. But as the screen dissolves, you find those ARMS ABOUT YOU. You can feel His breath on your neck. You've shifted from faith to fact — in a flash!

The apostle Paul knew this — and couldn't wait:

". . . I say, and prefer rather to be absent from the body and to be at home with the Lord" (2 Cor. 5:8 NAS).

He was aware of Jesus' presence on the other side of the mirror and couldn't wait for death to shatter the barrier and usher him into Jesus' literal presence.*

AND THEN

"When Christ, Who is your life, appears, then you also will appear with Him in glory" (Col. 3:4 NIV)!

One day a trumpet blast will shatter the heavens. Eyes will turn skyward to behold an awesome sight in the clouds. They'll behold a dazzling color pageant that outshines the sun! For there is Jesus — ALIVE! And we're with Him! As death shatters the mirror in our minds, this event shatters the space-time barrier. The Lord Jesus has stepped back into time, **bringing us with Him!** We cross back over with Him to participate in a long-awaited moment — the "marriage of the Lamb!"

Can you picture the joy on Jesus' face as He revels in the honor and praise of those who truly love Him; who were so overwhelmed by His sacrifice for them, **they**

---

*For an in-depth study of what happens at death and the fascinating details of our bodily resurrection, see the author's book, **DEATH: GRADUATION TO GLORY.** You'll be thrilled to learn the actual mechanics of the exciting adventure called death.

PUT HIM FIRST. Imagine how He'll feel looking around on those who came to know Him INTIMATELY BY FAITH and adore Him! What a delight for Him to be with ALL HIS BELOVED AT ONCE! He'll weep for joy.

This, dear friend, is the "joy that was set before Him" (Heb. 12:2). This is the biggest day of His entire life — far bigger than when He first heard the words, "This is My beloved Son" (Matt. 3:17). On this day Jesus will look back on all His suffering and exclaim, "IT WAS WORTH IT ALL!"

Standing there beaming with delight, you and I will be thrilled to see Him so happy. When His joy causes tears to stream down His face, it will be ecstasy for us to realize we helped bring Him that joy.

⁂✶✶

YOU NOW HAVE A SECRET YOU CAN'T KEEP

Some months ago I read of eight prospectors who set out in search of gold. They spent weeks in some of Arizona's most desolate mountains, enduring all kinds of hardships. The lure of a rich find kept them going long after they should have turned back. One by one, the men died off until only 2 remained. Discouraged, the two survivors decided to call it quits and go home.

On the way back they paused at a creek to refresh the horses. One of the men casually picked up a stone from the brook, thinking perhaps to hurl it. But something about it made him take a closer look. He called for a hammer. When the stone broke, pure nuggets fell into his hand.

"Hey look," he shouted wildly, **"we've got gold here!"**

Immediately the two were scrambling all about the creek. Within minutes they had turned up even bigger nuggets.

"We've struck it rich!" one of them yelled.

"Whoooooeeee, there's gold all over the place!" echoed the other.

They danced about crazily, shouting and firing their pistols into the air. For a few minutes they were out of their heads, insane with joy. Then . . .

"Shhhhhhh . . . we gotta be quiet about this. Let's get into town as fast as we can and file our claim. And when we get there, don't breathe one word about this to anyone."

Both agreed. They marked their claim and set out for the nearest town where they could file and get supplies. Guarding their lips and movements so as not to give away their secret, the two men secured what they needed and quickly headed out of town. They were eager to get back to their claim. But as they made their way into the hills, they were followed by several dozen people who also staked out claims nearby.

The two men feverishly worked their claim, extracting several million dollars in pure gold. Those staking adjacent claims got rich too. But it remained a puzzle as to why the discoverers had been followed. Later, one of those who had followed them explained the mystery. . .

"YOUR BEAMING FACES BETRAYED YOUR SECRET!"

The prospectors had stumbled onto a secret so great, their bodies couldn't conceal it. It didn't matter that they hadn't said a word. From the glow in their eyes and the joy in their expressions, people KNEW AT ONCE they'd made a big strike.

THE SAME WILL BE TRUE OF YOU

Have you heard of the PEG LEG mine in Arizona? It's been lost for years, but it is said to be one of the richest gold strikes in history. Some reports describe veins of pure gold running for great distances. Its wealth is estimated in billions rather than millions. Now, if you were to stumble across this fabled mine, you'd get pretty excited. It would be hard to sit on such a secret. Chances are, the glow in your face would give you away too.

Well, you've made a discovery of far greater value than the Peg Leg mine. **You've discovered how to minister to the Lord in the "secret place."** When Brother

Lawrence made this discovery, his radiance was such, the royalty of Europe came begging for his secret. People everywhere were talking about him, observing the way his obsession changed his countenance. They just had to know his secret.

The same will be true of you. The reality of Jesus will seize you, giving you a new PASSION FOR HIS PRESENCE, and everyone will see it. You won't be the same person. Friends will do a double-take when they behold the glow in your face! Some will exclaim, "You seem so different! What's happened to you?" You won't be able to direct them to the LOST PEG LEG MINE, but brother . . . sister . . .

WILL YOU HAVE A SECRET TO SHARE!

Epilogue

It's Hard To Say
Good-bye ...

"Let us rejoice and be glad
and give Him glory!
For the wedding of the Lamb has come,
and His bride has made herself ready!"
(Rev. 19:7 NIV)

This book could end with the last chapter and I would have said all I needed to say. Just look at the holy ground we've covered, the precious time we've had together. This has been an intimate experience. For us to go through what we've just shared has to make us close friends. For that reason, it's hard to say "Goodbye."

But we really don't have to. There are more good things we can explore together, more adventures like the one we've just had. In fact, I'd love to have you work with me in helping the "BRIDE" GET READY for Jesus' return. That's the burden of my heart, and if you spend much time in the "secret place," that same burden could rest on your heart, too.

So here's what I'd like to do; send you a GIFT COPY of my autobiography, C. S. LOVETT: MARANATHA MAN. I would like for you to read it and then see how you feel about working with me. Of course, if you already have a copy, you won't need this one. You'll already know what I'm trying to do for Jesus and how I'm going about it. If you're afraid I'm going to ask a lot from you, relax. **My primary interest in you is PRAYER. I'm sold on prayer as God's way of getting the job done.**

Plus no man gets the credit.

All you have to do to receive your free copy is write, saying . . .

"Brother Lovett, it was fabulous going with you into the 'secret place' and learning how to minister to the Lord. I too feel God's Spirit telling me we are in the final hours of this age. I'd like to know more about your vision and what I can do to help the 'bride' make herself ready for the Lord. So please send me a gift copy of L 5485 MARANATHA MAN. As I read

190

it, I'll be listening for the Spirit's witness to see if He
wants our friendship to develop further."

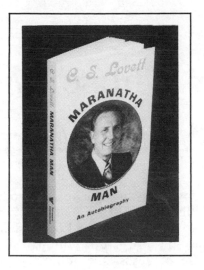

I realize it's unusual to have an author speak to you
personally after you've finished one of his books. But
this is PERSONAL CHRISTIANITY and I feel close to
those who love Jesus as I do. I'd like to have us go on
and become close friends. I don't want you to read the
book and forget me. There's a spiritual treasure and fellowship ahead for both of us — if we stick together and
pray for each other.

I'm convinced that once you read MARANATHA
MAN, the Spirit's witness will be so powerful, your
heart will beat with mine. You'll be writing back and
saying

"Wow, brother! This is fantastic! Let's get going!"

For Those Who Want More!

What follows may not be for everyone. It is for the "INNER CIRCLE" of believers who want to go deeper with the Lord and are willing to pay the price. For you MARYS, who want more of Jesus, the following sections (Appendix A and B) will bring you the ULTIMATE EXPERIENCE of faith.

This material is in the appendix, not because it is of less importance; but because I know the "inner circle" is small, perhaps 3 out of 12, as in the case of Peter, James and John. There is always a price on those things that bring the highest joy and deepest satisfaction. If you are one who is willing to pay the price, then what awaits you is an experience you never thought possible this side of heaven. To me it is the . . .

SUPREME ADVENTURE OF FAITH!

The Supreme
Adventure Of
The Faith Life

*". . . the Lord longs to be gracious to you, and therefore
He waits on high to have compassion on you . . .
How blessed are all those who long for Him."
(Isaiah 30:18 NAS)*

Here comes your teen-age daughter. She's all excited:

"Mother! Dad! The kids at church are having a weekend retreat in the mountains! Ken Poure is going to
minister. He's a super neat youth evangelist! Can I
go?"

Can she go? And how! You've been to youth confer-
ences. You know what a MOUNTAIN TOP experience
with the Lord is like! For a time, the flesh is powerfully
subdued and everything focuses on Jesus. Days at camp
are so filled with Christ, there's little place for the old
nature to assert itself.

You've seen young people return from these outings so on fire for Jesus they're beside themselves with enthusiasm and excitement. You've heard the thrilling testimonies of the decisions they've made. True, the enthusiasm wanes, but some deepening of the spiritual life remains.

THE BATTLE OF THE FLESH

As earth-bound creatures, we're used to dealing with that which we can see and touch. For us to enjoy a relationship with someone we can't see is a tremendous shift. It's a battle of faith vs. flesh.

For . . .

★ It's by faith that we enter the "secret place."

★ It's by faith that we hold the Lord in our arms.

★ It's by faith that we speak to Him.

★ It's by faith that we hear His reply.

As fleshly creatures, it's awkward for us to function by faith. We're used to the five senses. Consequently our surroundings are more real to us than things of the Spirit. If your husband or wife were to walk into the room right now and want to tell you something, you'd immediately put down the book and listen. That's because your mate is more real than ministering to the Lord — no matter how fantastic the discovery.

God knows all about this. He's well aware of the flesh's power to hinder. Did not Jesus say, "The spirit is willing, but the flesh is weak." (Mk. 14:38). So I doubt if you'll be surprised when I tell you He has provided a way to overcome fleshly opposition. However, you may be surprised at THE MEANS. You may not be ready for this. I doubt if you have a glimmer of what is coming.

God's method of subduing the flesh is every bit as effective as a mountain top experience at a youth retreat. And here it is . . . (hang onto your chair) . . .

FASTING!

Wait A Minute! Don't Panic!

To most of you, I know I just said a horrifying word. Terrible things can pop into a person's mind at the mention of fasting. Hunger . . . starvation . . . agony. Everything inside rebels at the thought. Well, in just a bit I'm going to tell you THREE THINGS ABOUT FASTING that should change your feelings.

Besides, it is SATAN who should panic. He knows what God does with fasting, and how **He's used it down through the centuries to empower his mightest servants!**

Fasting is a powerful spiritual weapon. The devil doesn't want it in the hands of God's people. **He trembles when believers mean business for Christ to the place where they will forego food to become intimate**

with Him. The person who puts Jesus ahead of food is dead serious. That's the price I was talking about. With our modern passion for food, this is a high price tag.

Yet when we look at the giants of the Bible; men such as Moses, David, Elijah and Daniel, we find fasting the key to their power with God. The devil has worked hard to keep Christians from rediscovering its power. Those who fast regularly to seek the Lord testify that after the fifth day their spiritual sensitivity soars dramatically. **They find themselves able to spend long hours in prayer, enjoying the Lord's presence in a way not otherwise possible.** God, it seems, is ready to draw close to those more interested in Him than in food.

OUR LORD FASTED AND PRAYED

© Linda Lovett 1975

Jesus fasted after He was led into the wilderness to be "tempted of the devil." He'd just come from the Jordan river where He had been baptized by John the Baptist. As He came out of the water, His Father confirmed from heaven that He was the Son of God. What awesome news! Any clues or foregleams He may have had before that time were suddenly confirmed.

His life was blasted into a new realm. He needed time to discuss this great revelation with His Father. Thus He was led into the wilderness where the significance of the announcement could sink in and be tested.

After His 40 day fast, He was ready for the devil's 3 temptations. The Lord resisted each of them, passing the test. Then the devil left Him and angels came and ministered to Him (Matt. 4:1-11). Now He was ready for the task of redeeming mankind.

● On one occasion, when the Lord's disciples found themselves powerless to cast out certain demons, they went to Him about it. "This kind," He replied, "goeth not out but by fasting and prayer" (Matt. 17:14-21 KJV). Drawing close to Jesus through fasting and prayer injects spiritual power into the life of the believer.

NEW TESTAMENT SAINTS FASTED
AND PRAYED

● Right after he was saved on the Damascus road, the apostle Paul fasted and prayed for three days. During that time, he was shut up in the presence of the Lord, for God had blinded him. There, in that sightless world, he reviewed all that had happened to him and became personally acquainted with Christ.

After the three days, the Spirit instructed a man named Ananias to go to Saul and lay his hands on him. Immediately the apostle regained his sight and was filled with the Holy Spirit. After being baptized, he went to the synagogues where he publically proclaimed Jesus (Acts 9:9-20).

● The early Christian prophets and teachers (among them: Barnabas, Simon called Niger, Lucius and Saul) gathered together at Antioch to fast and minister to the Lord as a group. While they were fasting and ministering, the Spirit gave them specific orders:

"Set Barnabas and Saul apart for Me, to do the work for which I have called them."

Then — after still more fasting and prayer, the congregation laid hands on them, and Barnabas and Saul were dispatched as the first Christian missionaries (Acts 13: 1-3).

● Fasting has a way of detaching us from the material world around us and fixing our eyes on God. Finite things fade from view when our thoughts are centered on Jesus alone. **When a man gets to the place where he prefers fellowship with Jesus to food, it brings a release of faith that won't come any other way.** In those moments he is able to trust God for things otherwise impossible as long as his vision was clouded by temporal things. The Lord becomes super real in those times.

WHAT I MEAN BY FASTING

FOR THE PURPOSE OF THIS BOOK, FASTING IS ABSTAINING FROM ALL FOODS, BUT CONTINUING TO DRINK WATER AS NEEDED.

Here now are the three things I promised earlier. I'm certain they will make a difference in your attitude toward fasting.

1. THERE IS NO HUNGER AFTER 48 HOURS. It takes that long for the body to metabolize (convert) the carbohydrates in your system. After that, your digestive system shuts down. When the digestive juices stop flowing, HUNGER VANISHES. Did you get that? Hunger disappears! When people fast for extended periods, say 40 to 60 days, they have NO HUNGER at all during that time. THE DESIRE FOR FOOD LEAVES. This is why plane crash victims have survived 6 weeks and longer on nothing but water. Fasting does not harm the body, it cleanses it.

2. YOU CAN'T HURT YOURSELF. If God Himself required fasting of His people, you know it can't be bad for a person. And if it is a blessing to God's people, you also know Satan will hate it. You do need to know this: FASTING IS NOT STARVATION. You do NOT STARVE when you fast. Your body simply feeds on STORED FOOD. It burns up the fats collected in the blood stream and in rolls about the body. It burns up cholesterol. It incinerates poisons and wastes gathered in the tissues and organs. God has so designed the body that it WILL NOT feed upon good tissue or muscle until the waste products and fats are consumed first. THEN HUNGER RETURNS to let you know it's time to end the fast. Your body WARNS YOU before starvation begins. When Jesus was tempted by the devil, HE DIDN'T BECOME HUNGRY until He had fasted for 40 days and 40 nights. It was THEN that hunger returned. The RETURN OF HUNGER is the body's signal to end the fast, for it is about to feed on good tissue. So there's plenty of warning.

3. THE FLESH BOTTOMS OUT AROUND THE 7th DAY. By the 7th day (though this varies with the individual) the cries of the flesh will have died down. The greeds and passionate desires, yes even the sex drives vanish and the SPIRITUAL SIDE SURFACES. You become spiritually sensitive. So sensitive, in fact, you have to be careful of dreams and visions. You have to be selective, discriminating, for in a high spiritual state it is easy to attach too much importance to them. When a person attains this spiritual HIGH GROUND, it is every bit as consuming and thrilling as a mountain top experience at a hill top retreat. You get just as high and close to the Lord — even higher. In this state, the Lord becomes so real you can reach out and "touch" Him.

THIS IS WHAT WE'RE AFTER

199

I want you to experience the 7th-10th day phenomenon. I want you to know what it is like to have your physical desires die down and your spiritual awareness rise to a peak. This SPIRITUAL HIGH is tremendous. Going into the "secret place" with your spiritual nature in command will give you, what I call, the **maximum faith adventure.** There's nothing like it.

I'm eager for you to HOLD JESUS IN YOUR ARMS — at least one time — **with your spiritual senses at their peak! With your flesh subdued and your awareness incredibly quickened, the Lord's presence will be so real it will overwhelm you.** Honestly, I know of nothing in the range of Christian experience to match it!

● The idea of fasting may be a shock. It "blows the mind" of many. I know that. This is because Satan has worked overtime in getting Christians to picture fasting as torture. One of his most effective techniques is causing believers to become obsessed with food. Today they'll drive 50 to 100 miles to eat at a berry farm or unusual restaurant. He has Christians so addicted to food, the idea of fasting is repulsive. Why does he do this? He realizes fasting is one of God's most powerful tools.

> **NOTE.** If the idea of fasting frightens you, you can be sure those feelings don't come from the Lord. I must tell you, you can go into the "secret place" and enjoy Jesus without fasting, but the experience is vastly superior when your flesh has been subdued and your spiritual awareness allowed to dominate. More importantly, however, is your attitude toward food. It is a real measure of the place Jesus holds in your thinking. If food is more important to you than He, what does that say for your commitment? If we put food ahead of Him, then He's NOT FIRST. And all of our statements about His being "Lord of all" become empty. If we really mean business for Jesus, we'll put Him ahead of food.

200

DOES THE EXPERIENCE LAST?

Once you achieve a state of HIGH SPIRITUAL AWARENESS and thrill to a vivid encounter with the Lord, will your spirit stay at that level? No. When you return to eating, your flesh will resume its dominance. That's the way things are when you live in a physical body. The world closes in again, and spiritual awareness fades. But I will say this . . .

WHILE THE ENTHUSIASM WANES, THE REALITY REMAINS!

Once you've thrilled to such an experience, you never forget it. You're never the same. **Enjoy the Lord in this manner ONE TIME, with your spiritual senses aflame, and you'll never get over it.** The presence of the Lord is so overpowering in those moments, the reality will delight you till you die. Even when your flesh has resumed control, your future trips to the "secret place" are never the same. They take on a different character.

AFRAID OF FASTING?

You might be tempted to shrug off the idea unless you know the fabulous results that follow. Even then you might think, "Man, that's too far out for me!" I understand your feelings. I felt the same way. I used to think anyone who suggested I fast was out of his head. But actually, there's nothing to fear. Far from being harmful, it's one of the most beneficial things you can do — **both spiritually and physically. To see the modern church shun this spectacular grace is tragic.** The loss of blessing and power is incalculable.

BLESSINGS. Not all Christians ignore fasting. There are some who fast, and for various reasons. Some fast for spiritual power. Others to gain control over their appetites. This is a remarkable weapon against overeating. Then there are those who fast for health reasons. The body, as you know, is marvelous in its design. Cleanse it by fasting and it will practically rebuild itself — like new. While all those are terrific blessings, I feel the subduing of the flesh and the emergence of the spirit is the **chief of blessings.** Certainly that is the way God uses it in the Word. In early days, fasting had an important place in the church. I feel it's time we recovered this abandoned blessing.

DO IT!

How awful to read a book like this, come to the HIGHEST POINT of the Christian experience and then find yourself saying, "Well, I don't know about that!" How tantalizing to the Lord. Wouldn't it be better to say "Hummmh, I never realized fasting was so great! Maybe I'd better consider it. Surely 10 days couldn't hurt me!"

HONESTLY, IT CAN'T HURT YOU

You're aware of the riots that took place in Northern Ireland. And how a number of Irish lads elected to starve to death as a protest against the British government. Do you recall how long it took for them to die by that means? Every one took more than 60 days. It takes a LONG TIME to die by starvation (as long as you have water). That's why the protesters chose that method. It kept them in the public eye many days before they finally expired. My point — a person has to go without food for a very long time before he does himself in.

So — I repeat — **there's no way you can hurt yourself with a 10 day fast.** A person has to fast weeks and weeks before he reaches the starvation stage. This is not to say you won't experience any discomfort. You might have WITHDRAWAL SYMPTOMS like with drugs. After all, many of us are seriously addicted to food. And the body can set up an awful howl when you withhold something to which it is addicted.

It's only right to tell you in advance that your body (like a spoiled brat) could kick up a real fuss when you deny it food. But that is a normal reaction, nothing to fear. And then there are others who will have no reaction whatsoever. The chemical differences in people make it possible for some to fast with no discomfort, while others have all kinds of withdrawal symptoms.

NOTHING TO FEAR

Even though I say there is nothing to fear, some readers will start fasting with all kinds of apprehension. Those same fears can create distressing symptoms BY THEMSELVES. Fear can create more problems than the body itself when denied food. On the other hand if a person is relaxed, knowing God is eager to bless him, he easily avoids many of the troublesome symptoms. So determine ahead of time NOT TO WORRY about your body. Don't panic should nausea or some aches and pains develop. They will pass. You're not hurting yourself. These are normal reactions that occur in some people when the body is denied food.

EVEN MORE IMPORTANT than aches and pains is the matter of the SPIRITUAL HIGH. If a person on his first fast is overly worried about hurting his body, he won't realize his spiritual senses are keenly aware. Preoccupation with the body can make him MISS the spiritual high altogether. Then he'll say to himself, "It didn't work." But it's not true. It did work, only he was too busy with his body to realize it.

SHOULD THAT HAPPEN TO YOU, DON'T GET DISCOURAGED. SIMPLY PLAN ON DOING ANOTHER TEN DAY FAST THE NEXT MONTH. IF YOU MISS THE SPIRIT-

UAL HIGH THE SECOND TIME, THEN DO ANOTHER TEN DAY FAST A MONTH LATER. DON'T GIVE UP. YOU'LL MAKE IT.

How do you feel about it now? Think you'd like to give it a try? All right, let's do it. That's next.

MEDICAL WARNING

GO TO YOUR DOCTOR FOR A PHYSICAL EXAMINATION BEFORE BEGINNING THE FAST. BE SURE TO ASK FOR A GLUCOSE-TOLERANCE TEST. DISCUSS WITH HIM ANY MEDICATION YOU ARE TAKING TO SEE IF YOU SHOULD DISCONTINUE IT OR FIND A SUBSTITUTE.

Appendix B

The Top Of The
ℳountain

". . . My food is to do the will of Him Who sent
Me, and to accomplish His Work." (John 4:34 NAS)

It's Monday morning. You've weighed the matter, considering the symptoms versus the blessings. You've decided to try the 10 day fast. The scale tips too far in favor of the blessings to say fasting is not for you. Besides, you know too much now. You'd never feel right until you checked it out and experienced the total reality of Christ — by faith.

GOOD FOR YOU

Satan lost that one. Now we can get down to business.

The weekend is behind you. Monday morning is a great time to start. Hopefully you've already begun to taper off, backing away from some things, instead of indulging in a final splurge. That will make things easier.

FIRST DAY

As you roll out of bed, talk to the Lord. That's the way to start:

"Good morning Father. This is the day You and I start subduing my flesh by denying it food. I'm new at this, so when my flesh howls, You'll have to help me give it a deaf ear. I ask You to strengthen me, to reinforce my determination. I commit my body into Your hands, knowing You will protect it. I also ask You to make me sensitive to the quickening of my spirit.

"Father, I expect this to be a fabulous experience for both of us. Help me to focus on You, rather than be concerned about my body.

And may it bring You great joy, dear Lord, to find me putting You ahead of food! I thank You in advance for what is about to happen. Amen!"

● You pause at the sink, your first stop in the kitchen. You're going to have a glass of water for breakfast. You'll be amazed how satisfying water can be. As we go along, you'll come to appreciate its power to take the edge off hunger. If you have to fix breakfast for the family, purpose not to touch one bite. You're going to go for 10 days with nothing but water.

A glass of water will do for breakfast. It's surprising how satisfying water can be.

WATER. The first hungers come in the afternoon. Addicted to food, your body will start to fuss. When it does, pour a glass of water and drink it slowly. Hunger attacks last for about 15 minutes. Water takes the edge off of them at once, helping you through the interval. The entire hunger span is approximately 48 hours, or until the carbohydrates in your body are consumed. Then the digestive system shuts down and hunger disappears. If you wish to drink weak coffee, that's okay. Should cramps or nausea develop, prepare a small glass of DILUTED orange juice and sip it slowly. Mix half-water and half-juice. Keep it in the refrigerator and use it sparingly. It can get you over any rough spots. If hunger persists after the 48 hours, this is usually phantom hunger, induced by Satan. Dealing with him can take care of that.

THE SECOND DAY

Your body starts to react, most do. The "spoiled brat" will begin kicking up a fuss. It's possible you will feel a few pains, again you may feel nothing. Some people sail through these fasts with no discomfort at all. As the supply of carbohydrate is used up, the body will start running on a stored fuel. It is inferior to food, but it burns good enough to keep you going at ¾ normal strength.

Stored fuel consists of the fats that cling to your body, wastes deposited in the organs, and even cholesterol collected in your arteries. Believe me, there's plenty of it in the average Christian.

Your body likes food. It's used to it. And when you shift to inferior fuel, it is going to protest. **But you're in charge.** Your body must do what you tell it, not the other way around. As soon as your body starts to fuss, Satan will taunt you with suggestions:

"You're crazy going through all this. Why don't you forget this nonsense and sit down to the table with

your family? You know they're going to think you've gone off the deep end. Besides, how do you know you're not damaging your body? You have but one body and God expects you to take care of it. It needs good food to function as God intends. Really, you should quit this."

You can count on the devil to bombard you with suggestions. If you buy his ideas, he'll have you believing you can hurt yourself. So take James' advice "RESIST HIM" (James 4:7). He'll back off. Sure, he'll wait for an unguarded moment and be right back. But that's part of the process. You simply resist him again.

"Satan, in the name of Jesus, take your suggestions and get out of here. I command you in His name to depart from me for it is written 'I will not be mastered by anything!' " (1 Cor. 6:12b)

When you fast, you're not simply fighting the flesh. The devil is keenly aware of the tremendous experience ahead of you and will do all he can to keep you from it. Fortunately, once the digestive system shuts down, he has less to work with. As I told you, this occurs when the carbohydrate in your body has been consumed, roughly 48 hours. What's more, once your spiritual nature begins to dominate, he'll be less inclined to tangle with you. He likes EASY victims.

THIRD DAY

By now you should notice a marked **decrease** in hunger. The system is shutting down. The flow of digestive juices is subsiding. The cries of the flesh are beginning to diminish. Things start to look up when you get to this point. You have a sense of power, able to look at food and say "Who needs it!" But — you do have to get past those first 48 hours. That's the toughest part. After that, it's downhill the rest of the way.

FOURTH DAY

By now your body is running on fat. If you're like most of us, you've got enough to keep going for weeks. Did you know there is AS MUCH FAT on the INSIDE of your body as there is on the OUTSIDE? If you can pinch rolls on the outside, you've got rolls on the inside, too. There's plenty of fuel on hand. I repeat that because Satan is going to tell you the opposite.

Weakness could begin on this day. Not a lot, but some. You see, the body doesn't run as well on LOW GRADE FUEL as it does on food. But that's not the only reason. At this point, your body is beginning to DETOXIFY itself. It is gathering up a lot of your wastes and toxins and throwing them in the furnace. You'll be coming up on what the experts call "the cleansing crisis." All kinds of poisons and accumulated wastes are being incinerated. You'll get a nice house cleaning out of this as a bonus.

FIFTH AND SIXTH DAYS

Let's say you experience weakness for 3 days. That'll take us through the 5th day. On the 6th day, you'll feel **strength beginning to return**. Isn't that amazing? You're fasting, yet getting stronger. That's because the cleansing is passing, releasing energy for other things. You won't be able to go full blast, as if you were eating, but you'll function at ¾ of your original strength.

> **WEAKNESS.** If your job is such that this weakness will seriously affect your performance, then you'll need a bit of help, something to get you past the interval. Take a quarter lemon and squeeze the juice into a small 4 oz. glass. Add water to fill it. Then add ¼ teaspoon of honey and stir. Honey, already digested by the bees, will go directly into your blood stream. You'll feel the boost of power, but this tiny amount of carbohydrate will NOT fire up your digestive system and end the fast. Use it sparingly, only enough to help you over the hump. If you do hard, manual work, then you probably shouldn't fast at all. Burning fat as fuel may not supply the strength you need for your job. But for most occupations it should be plenty.

● I should warn you that pregnant women and nursing mothers should NOT FAST. Why? **Because of the cleansing crisis.** All of the poisons and waste picked up by the blood stream will flow through the fetus and also be in the nursing mother's milk.

If you are taking medication, by all means check with your doctor. Some medicines double and triple their potency when taken without food. In fact, if you suspect a medical condition in your body, it would be wise to ask your doctor about it. But don't expect him to approve of fasting. Most won't. Most doctors are not trained in nutrition and health. Their schooling, it seems, is restricted to sickness and disease. I don't say that to put them down. Doctors are God's gift to us when we need them.

WEIGHT LOSS. Please don't go on this fast for the purpose of losing weight. While you will lose weight, possibly as much as 2 lbs. a day, that is not the purpose. Look on that as merely a nice by-product. We have a much nobler ambition, **drawing close to Jesus at a time when our spiritual awareness reaches its peak.** There is, however, another phenomenon that might surprise you — when hunger vanishes, there may be times when the fragrance of food will make you nauseous. I'll bet you never thought that could happen.

NOW FOR THE SPIRITUAL SIDE

DAYS 1 — 6: As your body goes through the initial phases of fasting (hunger, diminished hunger, weakness, returning strength) and you are approaching the spiritual high, do all you can to prepare the INNER MAN, the "new man," as Paul calls him. **As you DENY food to the outer man, INTENSIFY the feeding of the INNER MAN.** You know, time in the Word, and being alone with the Lord. At mealtime, when your family is feasting on food, retire to a solitary place and fill your soul with the "Bread of Life."

Just as you prepare your body for fasting by backing away from food, so can you prepare your soul for feasting, by **indulging in the Word of God.** The inner man loves HIS FOOD as much as the outer man loves his. Taking time to feed on the Word and fellowship with the Lord conditions you for the super experience just ahead. You'll be ready for it, anticipating it.

Do you have breaks and lunch periods at work? Use that time for spiritual refreshment. Devote the time you would normally spend feeding the outer man to feeding the inner man. That's a fair trade-off. You'll find that as your flesh dies down and your spiritual nature ascends, all sorts of insights will start breaking across your mind as you open the Word. It's exciting to prepare the inner man for what is coming.

212

As you deny food to the outer man, intensify the feeding of the inner man by indulging in the Word of God. This conditions you for the super experience just ahead.

DAYS 7 — 8: Isn't it just like the Lord to make the 7th day special! On this day your flesh is quiet. Your carnal appetite is gone. Your earthly desires have vanished. I mean even greeds, hostile feelings and sexual impulses. They all disappear. There's nothing to match this. You can't believe how spiritual you feel. And when you talk to the Lord, you just know you can reach out and touch Him. You lose track of time in His presence — it's overpowering.

Days pass quickly now. There is no hunger. Your flesh is dominated by your spirit. **You are filled with the joy of the Lord. You're almost to the top of the mountain.** Again and again you go into the "secret place," thrilling to fantastic times with the Lord. Wow! Is He real to you! And when you press your cheek next to His, well, I doubt if it will be any more blessed when you meet Him in the air! What a "love affair!" — You and the Lord — in the SPIRIT!

> **VISIONS.** It seems almost irreverent to utter a caution when we're on such high ground, but I need to say this: when you're spiritually high, you become sensitive to the spiritual realm. As you know, there are lots of "principalities and powers" out there. You could easily receive a vision. Those that truly exalt the Lord Jesus will be from God. Any that exalt YOU will not be from God. You may see yourself in some fantastic role, but watch out. Satan would like to use this super experience against you and get you OFF ON A TANGENT. DON'T MAKE CHANGES IN YOUR DOCTRINE, LIFE WORK OR PERSONAL RELATIONSHIPS based on visions alone. Check everything against the Word. Because of your super sensitivity, you may hear "other voices."

 You're sitting in church. Your Bible is in your lap as you listen to your pastor speak, "Let's turn to Hebrews Thirteen and read a wonderful passage together." Your eyes drink in the precious words as he reads aloud,

> **"The Lord said, 'I will never leave thee, nor forsake thee. So that we may boldly say, The Lord is my Helper, and I will not fear what man shall do unto me' "** (vss. 5,6).

He continues, "And the reason we know He will never forsake us is found in another wonderful verse:

214

'. . . he who unites himself with the Lord is one with Him in Spirit' " (1 Cor. 6:17 NIV).

Aren't those glorious words? Don't you thrill to them? Let me tell you it is one thing to read them in church, quite another to **hear them from the Lord Himself.** To have Him hold you in His arms and say, "I will never leave you nor forsake you," will send your soul into ecstacy. Taste that delirious joy and you won't want to leave the "secret place."

DAYS 9 & 10: THE TOP OF THE MOUNTAIN. Congratulations! Praise the Lord! You've made it to the top. You've reached the peak of spiritual awareness, going as far as one can go in the body. For the past two days, you've been basking in His presence, delighting in His love. **Now you're going to use the remainder of your time ministering to His needs.**

To go into the "secret place" with your spirit aflame and minister to Jesus, is, in my opinion, THE SUPREME ADVENTURE OF FAITH! The thrill is indescribable. I can no more tell you what it is like than Paul could describe what it was like to be caught up to the "third heaven" (2 Cor. 12:1-4). You'll just have to experience it for yourself. But I assure you, you'll never be the same. Your obsession with Jesus will become a volcano in your soul.

You're going to end the fast at TEN DAYS. Why 10 days? Because it keeps you well within safe limits, and you've accomplished what you set out to do. In actual practice you may feel like going on. It's easy when there's NO HUNGER. And that **no hunger** condition lasts until all your stored reserves are used up. Then hunger returns. That's the signal (the alarm) the body sounds to let you know it's time to stop fasting. But a 10 day fast is enough for now.

BREAKING THE FAST

This is important. It's a lot easier to GO ON a fast than to COME OFF one. While a 10 day fast is not all that critical, I should mention three big changes that have occurred:

(1). Your stomach has shrunk below its normal size, and the gastric juices have ceased to flow.

(2). The organs used for digesting food (stomach/intestines) have gone into hybernation.

(3). A totally different energy process has been activated as your body shifted from a FOOD-BURNING to a FAT-BURNING machine.

All that must now return to normal. With the stomach awakening from its nap, it is not ready for SOLID FOOD. It will take about 4 days to get things back to normal. Nearly every authority on fasting agrees the safest way to break a fast is with either fruit or vegetable juices.

Orange juice is fine, apple juice even better, tomato juice or grape juice will do. DON'T USE MILK. It's harder to digest and isn't easily processed in the lower intestine, expecially if you drink a lot at once. Some people have trouble with milk after a fast. If you're one who likes milk, give yourself a few days before trying it.

FIRST DAY

Awaken your digestive system with ONE-FOURTH glass of diluted fruit or vegetable juice. Again add equal amounts of water. You now have half a glass of liquid. Be sure it is room temperature. Don't gulp it — **sip it**. Though you've only fasted 10 days, you could induce cramps by downing four ounces at once. Stay on juices throughout the first day.

SECOND DAY

On the second day, you can enjoy some soup. It will taste good. Toward evening, a bit of melon, or grapefruit, or an orange. Chew it well. If bloating occurs, return to the juices for another 12 hours.

THIRD DAY

Breakfast can include any of the fresh fruits in season. But don't overindulge. The stomach isn't ready to handle too much. If you feel you are overworking it, back off. Go back to juices for the remainder of your meal. A baked apple would be fine now.

Lunch can include a very small fresh vegetable salad. Don't use any dressing, but if it seems too flat, put some lemon juice on it. A cooked, non-starchy vegetable (leafy greens) could be added. Doesn't sound like much of a meal, but your stomach isn't going to want much right now. Try a little cottage cheese with your salad. Good protein.

FOURTH DAY

Fruit again for breakfast. Lunch can now include a salad or baked potato. Or make that a baked apple, if you like. Protein may be introduced in the form of cheese or eggs if your body is accepting food well.

Fresh fruits are on your dinner menu again, and toasted whole grain bread may be eaten with a thin scraping of butter. You can try some milk, preferably raw, nonfat milk. If you experience discomfort from the milk, return to juices, skipping the next meal if you don't feel like eating

FIFTH DAY

From here on, play it by ear. The 5th day should see your eating habits go back to normal. If you're overdoing it at any time, your body will let you know. You're going to feel as though you have a new body as well as a new intimacy with the Lord.*

THE ULTIMATE EXPERIENCE

You've tasted heaven, at least as much as anyone can in the body. **You've come to within A STEP of the actual presence of the Lord.** With your flesh subdued by the fast and your spiritual sensitivity at its zenith, you've achieved the supreme experience of faith. Having put Jesus ahead of food, you have experienced an INTI-

---

* I realize these details could seem a little skimpy, but they'll do since you're only going to fast for 10 days. You're not likely to get into any real trouble. If you have qualms about fasting for 10 days or feel uneasy about denying food to your body, you should probably refer to my book, **"HELP LORD — THE DEVIL WANTS ME FAT!"** A good portion of that book is devoted to taking you through this fast, day by day, as well as resisting Satan's temptations.

MACY with Him known to few Christians. You now belong to the "inner circle."

• Should you find yourself on the receiving end of the wrath of antichrist, you can easily run into the "secret place" and into those "everlasting arms." If death strikes your body while you're holding Jesus in your arms, you won't be aware of it. As the mirror/screen in your mind fades, you LITERALLY FIND YOUR-SELF in His arms. All death can do to you is . . .

TURN YOUR FAITH INTO FACT!

NAME _____ DATE STARTED _____

DAILY DELIGHT CHART

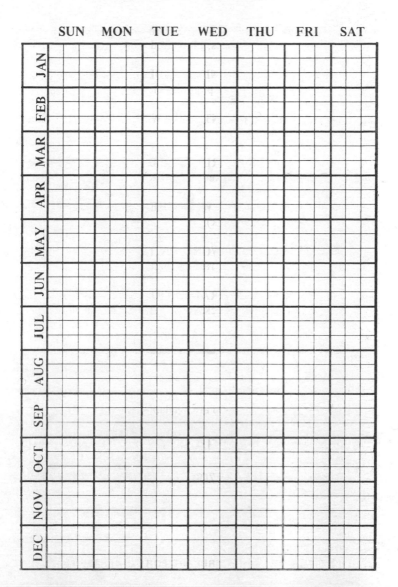

	SUN	MON	TUE	WED	THU	FRI	SAT
JAN							
FEB							
MAR							
APR							
MAY							
JUN							
JUL							
AUG							
SEP							
OCT							
NOV							
DEC							

NAME _____ DATE STARTED _____

MINISTERING TO THE
LORD'S 5 NEED AREAS

WK.	NEEDS	S	M	T	W	T	F	S
1								
2								
3								
4								
5								